EARTH WARRIOR

• • •

EARTH WARRIOR

• • •

OVERBOARD
WITH PAUL WATSON
AND THE
SEA SHEPHERD CONSERVATION SOCIETY

DAVID B. MORRIS

Fulcrum Publishing
Golden, Colorado

Cover design by Companion Press, Santa Barbara, California
Interior design by Jane Hopkins

Cover photos courtesy of the Sea Shepherd Conservation Society, Santa Monica, California.

Cover map courtesy of the Oregon Historical Society, #OrHi 90848.

Excerpt from "For the Children" in *Turtle Island* by Gary Snyder. Reprinted by permission of New Directions Publishing Corp.

Excerpt from "In Blackwater Woods" from *American Primitive* by Mary Oliver. Copyright © 1983 by Mary Oliver. First appeared in *Yankee* magazine. Reprinted by permission of Little, Brown and Company.

Library of Congress Cataloging-in-Publication Data
Morris, David B.
Earth warrior: overboard with Paul Watson and the Sea Shepherd Conservation Society / David B. Morris.
p. cm.
ISBN 1-55591-203-6
1. Watson, Paul. 2. Edward Abbey (Ship) 3. Sea Shepherd II (Ship) 4. Marine mammals. 5. Wildlife conservation. I. Title.
QL31.W34M67 1995
333.9516'092—dc20 94-37952
CIP

Printed in the United States of America
0 9 8 7 6 5 4 3 2 1

Fulcrum Publishing
350 Indiana Street, Suite 350
Golden, Colorado 80401-5093

To the memory of
Elizabeth Allston Morris

stay together
learn the flowers
go light

—Gary Snyder, "For the Children"

CONTENTS

• • •

PREFACE

• • •

On June 21, 1993, the summer solstice and the longest day of the year, Elizabeth Morris was driving her sixteen-year-old nephew, Jason, back from a visit to the University of Maine, where she held the position of Protestant campus minister. She had lived in Maine for three years, her first ministry, and in that brief time an entire community had come to recognize and respect the willowy young woman in her mid-forties as she raced around campus with her unmistakable roan-red hair, bright eyes, gentle smile and passion for social justice. Her nephew had come for a visit and to hear a reading by legendary American poet Allen Ginsberg. Now she was driving him back to his home in Vermont.

As Elizabeth drove south along the Maine turnpike, a football-sized chunk of concrete from an overpass—thrown down or perhaps flipped over the rail by a passing truck—smashed through her windshield and killed her instantly. Jason somehow escaped serious injury as the car rammed into an embankment.

Elizabeth was my sister. She was also, as I have come to learn, a woman whose spirit—always striving and indomitable—touched a great many people from Maine to California. As she wrote in one of her sermons, "Spirit means breath, and spirituality can be seen in a person who is full up with the breath of life, full of vitality and a love of life." She understood her own spiritual life as deeply connected to the earth.

She loved to camp, to walk outdoors, to sit in a field or under a tree, playing her flute. The earth—finite, enduring, magnificent—was a source of strength to her, even when what she called the "amazing days" it gives us turned dark. In her role as minister, Elizabeth sometimes shared with grieving families the final lines from Mary Oliver's poem "In Blackwater Woods":

> To live in this world
>
> you must be able
> to do three things
> to love what is mortal;
> to hold it
>
> against your bones knowing
> your own life depends in it;
> and, when the time comes to let it go,
> to let it go

Elizabeth would understand why someone might love the mortal earth with a fierceness that could not bear to watch it carelessly destroyed.

Canadian-born environmental activist Paul Watson is someone whose passion Elizabeth would value. What follows is the account of my voyage with Watson on an antidriftnet campaign in the North Pacific during the summer of 1992. The account weaves together in a single narrative three main strands: the voyage, its ecological context and a gradually emerging sketch of Paul Watson. Watson matters, whether you admire or despise him, because he puts us so clearly on notice that the time for inaction or halfway measures is over. His way of life and way of thinking challenge us to question our ingrained attitudes and actions. At his most impressive, he offers a compelling example of what a new human relationship to the earth could be.

This is a personal book, and I think it has to be personal. My own unheroic role as narrator—a middle-aged writer, scholar and ex-professor so clearly out of his element—is something I cannot help. One reason for not washing out my role in later rewritings is to preserve something of the individual education that went on during the voyage and its aftermath. The point is that we all need to educate ourselves about the environment, and such learning will always be individual and personal. What we learn most deeply will not be abstract theories or a set of facts but something that, if we let it, is likely to touch us, disturb us and possibly change us forever.

In the last two hundred years the earth has come under an accelerated assault that has changed it forever. The evidence is all around us in smokestacks, dams, nuclear reactors, megacities blazing deep into space. Species are going extinct at rates never before known. The earth, of course, has continued to change throughout its 4- or 5-billion-year history: mountain ranges rise and fall, continents drift apart, ice ages come and go. The recent changes are unprecedented, however, in the sense that they are almost entirely caused by humans. And, though humans have always altered their environment—burning woods, digging roots, domesticating crops or animals—never during the forty thousand years it took *Homo sapiens* to spread across the earth has such change come so fast, never on such an enormous scale and absolutely never in ways that could produce a global catastrophe.

It is difficult to think about these changes, about what they mean and about what we should do. It is difficult to grasp the loss we see all around us as suburbs sprawl and condominiums rise. Perhaps my personal difficulties are finally no more than a metaphor. Learning that runs counter to deeply set patterns is always a struggle and often a journey. My journey with Paul Watson, I now sense, still has far to go.

CHAPTER ONE

THE APPOINTMENT

• • •

Paul Watson is not what I had expected. Sea captains evoke for my landlocked midwestern imagination lean, bearded, taciturn figures, hard around the eyes (from all that squinting at the horizon) and ramrod stiff, like cops with wisdom. But Watson is no ordinary captain. He is founding director of the Sea Shepherd Conservation Society, and the stories he inspires make you think of guerrilla fighters—outgunned rebels who launch bold, sudden assaults against the armies of a colonial empire. So my expectations ran to something like Abraham Lincoln in combat fatigues or a tall, handsome Yasser Arafat. But the man who pulled up to berth 147 in a plum-colored Toyota Supra looked more like a stocky, if imposing, nineteenth-century impressionist painter. His thick, tangled, silver-black hair curling halfway down his neck and his blue pirate-style shirt open to midchest seemed almost shocking in their excess, even here at the Port of Los Angeles in the land of movie stars.

What struck me immediately as we shook hands beside the all-black, ninety-five-foot, decommissioned Coast Guard cutter—renamed the *Edward Abbey*—was his mix of vigilance and utter calm. He seemed to take in everything at a glance, leaving me with the impression that I had just been fingerprinted, frisked for weapons and cross-checked with the radical equivalent of Interpol. His was an air of confident strength. His stout lower jaw looked like it would see a prizefighter through a hard career.

Although two hours late, he apologized with the friendly nonchalance of someone who regards appointments as at best a social fiction. So what if the midday sun appeared to slide a few degrees toward the horizon while I hung around the docks waiting? His calm seemed to suggest that only creatures saturated in illusion could believe that clocks count for much. After all, it wasn't the sun that had moved but rather the tilted, spinning earth we stand on. Yet his greeting also had a curious openness about it.

My handshake with Paul Watson felt like the end of a journey. I had been trying to contact him sporadically for several years, ever since my wife and I first saw his ominous black ship, the *Sea Shepherd II*, moored, or perhaps quarantined, at a fenced-off dock in Key West. Evidently Watson is not a very reliable correspondent. Several friends had told me that he generally keeps his whereabouts secret. (They were badly mistaken, it turns out.) For a while, discouraged, I stopped trying to reach him, but then almost by chance I received a Los Angeles telephone number to call. I happened to be in L.A. on a book tour when the number arrived, and it was with something like astonishment that I heard Paul Watson answer the phone. We arranged to meet at the docks in San Pedro, near Long Beach, and so here I am.

⚓ ⚓ ⚓

There's a grain of truth in the story that Paul Watson keeps his whereabouts hidden. Many Americans haven't heard of him—he might as well be living in secret—but outside America he is widely known as an important environmental activist. He is one of the founders of Greenpeace. He invented the tactic of tree-spiking to save old-growth forests from lumber companies. He has disrupted government-sanctioned wolf hunts and seal hunts—getting arrested, beaten up and nearly killed for his trouble. With his 189-foot, 657-ton converted cod trawler, *Sea Shepherd II*, he has rammed Japanese driftnet ships a thousand miles from land. He has confronted Russian whalers on the high seas and been pursued by helicopter gunships.

"Any whaling ship on the ocean," he says matter-of-factly, "is a target for the Sea Shepherd Conservation Society."

In other words, for over twenty years, since the birth of the modern environmental movement in the early 1970s, Paul Watson has repeatedly put his life on the line to stop the destruction of marine wildlife and ocean habitat. His methods get him routinely denounced as a terrorist, but future generations may regard him as a hero—or, depending on what future they inherit, a tragic hero. Controversial, complex and enigmatic, he is someone whose impassioned defense of whales, seals, seabirds, dolphins and almost every form of endangered marine species marks him as a distinctive and—in a solitary way—representative figure of our time.

⚓ ⚓ ⚓

Turning aside briefly from our initial greeting, Paul excuses himself and deftly climbs aboard the *Edward Abbey* to hug a slim young woman with light blond hair who earlier introduced herself to me as Beth Larsen. Beth has just emerged from the bridge, cellular phone in hand, talking nonstop. She strikes me as a born talker, not just sociable but someone for whom protracted silence would be like death. As she and Paul attend to various details, I find my thoughts retracing the last few hours that brought me here.

My emotions had played havoc with the concentration needed for map-reading as I drove down the crowded Harbor Freeway on my way to the Port of Los Angeles. As I steered a borrowed, sluggish Buick Regal through the minefield of L.A. freeway construction, I couldn't help feeling that the bleak industrial landscape was an especially unlikely place to meet an environmentalist. My somewhat edgy commute terminated at the harbor in San Pedro, a place of warehouses and grey cement, where a few scrawny, marooned palm trees poke their heads over high-tension wires. The immense four-story cranes towering above the docks looked like one-legged prehistoric beasts—steel skeletons stranded beside the wide, soot-blackened beds of railroad tracks, frozen in some unnoticed extinction. My directions said to turn left at The Port Cafe, but I was not gaining confidence. The Port Cafe looked not just empty or closed but abandoned, with no sign of life except an old battered car parked alongside and two grease-stained workers (or perhaps vagrants) in old battered clothes.

At irregular intervals, a piercing, dockside loudspeaker barked out unintelligible electronic commands.

Berth 147 was not easy to find. At last, as I turned onto a hot asphalt strip running alongside water brackish with oil slicks, I got my first look at the *Edward Abbey,* its deck cluttered with dismantled machinery, riding so low that it seemed hidden in comparison to the mammoth freighters loading nearby, vast container ships with archaic names like *London Victory*. Moored at this remote, forlorn stretch of concrete dock, the *Edward Abbey* looked as abandoned as The Port Cafe.

The ship also had the slightly sinister look of a sleek black motorcycle waiting outside a bar. The white insignia hand-

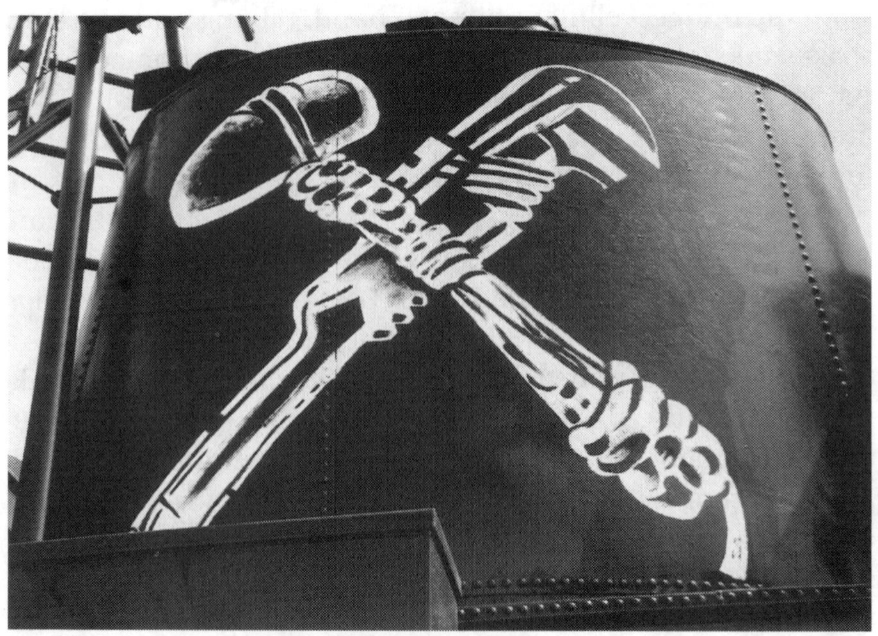

The tomahawk/monkeywrench insignia on the *Edward Abbey*

painted on its squat, cylindrical smokestack—a crossed monkey wrench and tomahawk—seemed to issue a belligerent if not quite comprehensible challenge. My eyes were drawn across the choked industrial waterway to the orange-tiled roofs of southern California bungalows climbing the crowded hillside as if straining for a glimpse of the sea. I tried to imagine the landscape as it had appeared to the first European explorers just a few hundred years ago. F. Scott Fitzgerald's words—"the fresh, green breast of the new world"—came to mind, but California has been turned green by sprinklers and irrigation ditches, and today even the palm trees looked a little tawdry. Just beyond the hillside, however, out of sight but marking everything with its scent and feel, was the Pacific Ocean, stretching westward for two thousand miles with no more than a few islands to interrupt its majestic sweep. It was the same ocean that Cortez had gazed upon, awestruck and silent, perhaps knowing he had come face-to-face with the ultimate image of mystery, openness and the unknown.

The two unkempt male figures who seemed attached to the *Edward Abbey,* coming and going at random, paid no attention to me. Finally I asked one of them—a frail young man with a fringe of yellow beard—if Paul Watson was around. He moved away without reply. A few minutes later, a young woman emerged from the ship, apparently appointed spokesperson, who said she was the cook. She assured me that Paul hadn't arrived yet. Soon they, too, left, and I spent my time mostly keeping out of the sun and trading occasional remarks with the one person aboard the *Edward Abbey* who seemed a permanent fixture. A thick-set man in his late twenties, covered with freckles and engine grease, he introduced himself as the chief engineer. At intervals he would shout a few friendly, inexplicable comments in my direction—machine-gun bursts of speech—and then, just as abruptly, disappear below deck.

His name was Scamp—no last name—just Scamp. The name seemed a misnomer for such a powerful, beefy figure whose sun-bleached strawberry hair straggled down over his eyes like a mask. He flashed the good-natured grin of someone who can't quite understand why he keeps ending up in trouble. Having evidently just finished up a lengthy repair job, he asked if I'd like to see the engines.

Climbing down onto the *Edward Abbey* from the dock felt like jumping into a hole. Clearly proud of the twin diesel engines he tended, Scamp took me down the steep staircase to the engine room so I could admire them close-up. The two massive diesel engines seemed to fill up the entire space with bulky red metal, making it almost impossible to turn around, while a maze of overhead pipes and dials inspired the vague sense of something about to explode. I agreed they were beautiful engines and hastily ascended to the sun.

Eventually Beth Larsen arrived. She sat down beside me on the long wooden bench as if we were old friends and smiled. "Hi, darlin'." She was not just outgoing, self-confident and spirited but also extremely practical: after some furious number-punching at her cellular phone she confirmed that Paul was just a few exits north on the freeway and would arrive soon. Beth, I later learned, calls everyone "darlin'," but her greeting made me feel a little less alien as I waited in the shade by a broken cable spool, trying to keep the grease off my sports jacket.

Promptness may be a minor virtue, but a virtue nonetheless. My private hell is a place where nobody ever shows up on time. I expected that an encounter with Paul Watson might require some hanging around and was prepared to wait, but the extended delay and the rundown dock had begun to grow wearisome. The public restroom, a few hundred feet away, was so clogged and smeared with filth that I fled outside. Not long afterward, the internal debate began in earnest about how much longer to wait.

At the moment I began to lean decisively toward leaving, the improbable plum-colored sports car pulled up alongside the dock.

⚓ ⚓ ⚓

Maybe time unfolds for Paul Watson the way it unfolds for a river or a flower—in seasons and long, slow rhythms. After spending a few minutes talking with Beth, he saunters over and sits down beside the large overturned spool that serves as a table. I give him the details I left out of our brief telephone call and explain my interest in the Sea Shepherd Conservation Society, which Paul founded some fifteen years earlier—in August 1977, to be exact. After a few more minutes I finally work up the nerve to say that I hope one day to come along on a voyage and write a book about the campaign.

Paul appears to let my statement linger in the air so that its absurdity can slowly achieve full blossom. Then he almost takes my breath away.

"We're leaving tomorrow. You're welcome to come along."

I've been told that I suffer from the flaw of backpedaling: I tend to rush ahead, following my emotions at breakneck pace, and then two days later I go full speed in reverse. It's not an attractive trait, but I'm stuck with it. The question that faces me now is whether, after finally meeting Paul Watson and getting invited to join a Sea Shepherd campaign, I will mull over my appointment book and pedal furiously backward. I can imagine myself saying something like, "I'm sorry. I guess I can't this time. Maybe later."

Fortunately there is a grace period. *The Edward Abbey,* Paul explains, will leave L.A. tomorrow and rendezvous with the *Sea Shepherd II* at Santa Cruz. Both ships will stay in Santa Cruz a few days for final provisions, so I could still join the campaign if I managed to reach Santa Cruz by Sunday. My series of radio interviews will end Friday afternoon in Seattle. A plane ticket and a little luck would get me to Santa Cruz. My summer schedule of speaking engagements, however, creates a more difficult problem because Paul can give no clear estimate of when we would return. He says we'll be somewhere in the North Pacific going after driftnet ships—"probably" for "about" a month, or until our fuel runs out. So much for precision. I tell him I'll try to rearrange my schedule, wondering how I can possibly manage it, and he gives me his Sky Page number.

A radical environmentalist with a Sky Page number?

"We'll look for you on the docks at Santa Cruz at 10:00 on Sunday morning," Watson says, no doubt a concession to my linear thinking, as he turns back to the *Edward Abbey.*

While we were talking, the deck filled up with duffel bags, parkas and large split-open boxes of potatoes.

I drive back to L.A. crossing beneath two unfinished overpasses that leave the elevated freeway stopping abruptly in midair. What should I do? I immediately get lost, of course, finding my way just in time to drop off the Buick, grab a beer and catch the airport shuttle to San Francisco. Over the next few days I spend time on the telephone with Ruth. She isn't crazy about my suddenly vanishing into the North Pacific for an unspecified period on a risky trip. My timing, moreover, is terrible. I would be leaving her alone in Ann Arbor to struggle with an accelerated graduate course in statistics. I have serious doubts as I recall the *Edward Abbey* with its disappearing ragtag crew and deck cluttered with junk. The dangers seem quite real. On the other hand, who knows when I might get another chance to join Paul Watson? A schedule is sometimes a socially acceptable excuse to hide behind. Am I really just afraid?

Ruth and I both secretly know I will go, but we continue to play out the charade of weighing pros and cons as I make my appointed stops up the coast. Seattle brought us to a decision. I squeeze in my final radio interview at the University of Washington between last-minute trips to the campus store. After mailing home most of my clothes, which would be useless on the open sea, I buy a tape recorder, camera, five hardcover lab books, a white baseball cap and a nylon windbreaker. Seasick patches require a doctor's prescription, so I load up instead with Dramamine tablets, adding, in a spasm of precaution, five bottles of sunblock and a first-aid kit. A nearby camping store finishes off my preparations with a flashlight, poncho and bargain-priced sleeping bag. Soon I'm back at my hotel, packed, stunned and ready to go.

After a restless night, I rise early and catch the first flight to San Jose—only a short ride by van, I was assured, from Santa Cruz. Who knows? It's all new to me.

⚓ ⚓ ⚓

The plane ride from Seattle to San Jose passes over a cloud cover so thick that it leaves nothing to see and offers a welcome chance for reflection. The episode that finally shook me out of my long sleep concerning the environment, I recall, was not the disasters at Bhopal or Chernobyl, not the massive Exxon oil spill in Alaska, not even the well-publicized claims about global warming. Oddly, it was the relatively innocuous moment in July 1988 when clumps of medical waste—syringes, IV tubing, hypodermic needles and vials of blood—began washing up on New Jersey beaches.

I grew up in Delaware, not far from the Jersey shore, drove as a teenager to the erotic surfside boardwalks and camped on the dunes along the Atlantic Ocean. I never wondered what happened to the soiled bandages and tongue depressors that my father tossed out routinely in his medical practice. It came as a big surprise to learn that hospitals, labs and nursing homes in New York State alone produce some 2 million pounds of infectious waste—each week. In the summer of 1988 the sea had apparently choked on the accumulating human rubbish and started to spew it back.

Why should medical waste have made the difference? Maybe the vials of blood and IV tubing expressed, in vivid images, something about the limits of nature. I can still picture it: the hot, sandy Jersey seashore, mottled with colorful umbrellas and a dense patchwork of beach towels, awash in a litter of syringes and blood-filled vials. The image is linked in my memory with the farcical barge *Mobro,* which, starting its journey in March 1987, sailed some six thousand miles in six months on a futile search for permission to unload its cargo of New York City garbage.

A few years later, in 1991, the Center for Marine Conservation organized volunteers to spend one day cleaning up the coastlines of America. On that single day, volunteers logged in 2.5 million pounds of trash. The U.S. Environmental Protection Agency reports that each American resident produces well over one thousand pounds of solid waste each year.

Certainly we have begun to reach some sort of limit. Since the start of the Industrial Revolution just 250 years ago, the human population has reproduced at jackrabbit speed from a few million people in 1700 to 5.6 billion in 1994. The UN predicts that early in the next century, the world population will double again, to 11 billion. Who can calculate the impact on the planet of 11 billion people? Maybe we should try to imagine twice as many cities, twice as many garbage dumps, twice as much poverty, crime, war and pollution.

When the figures get high enough, however, doubling doesn't just make a bad situation twice as bad. It goes from bad to instant nightmare. Suppose that each year the number of cars in America doubles. At first the numbers are insignificant: two cars, four cars, eight cars. Finally, one year the roads will be exactly half-full of cars—crowded, irritating, but maybe acceptable. The very next year, exponential doubling will produce sudden, total, bumper-to-bumper gridlock. Nothing moves, no space anywhere, everything simply grinds to a halt overnight. Exponential change is the nuclear warhead of mathematics.

Who is at fault? It doesn't work to hang all the blame on technology or industrialism or the usual abstract villains. I think back to the ancient stone ruins in the canyons of Arizona and New Mexico, where thriving Indian civilizations suddenly and mysteriously vanished. Experts now believe that they simply exhausted their environment: supplies of food, fuel and water just ran out. New York, Dallas and Los Angeles might one day lie similarly vacant in the wake of environmental overshoot: skyscrapers empty, reservoirs dry, computers down, pigeons dead, phones out.

The problem, then, seems to stretch beyond the laundry list of abuses that science could fix or, conceivably, that enlightened government could regulate. "Ban CFCs." "Clean the air." "Save the rain forest." The so-called solutions we cobble together often just disguise or delay the catastrophe. For example, after the Jersey beaches filled up with medical waste, the resulting public outcry pushed Congress—yes, it was an election year—to pass the Ocean Dumping Ban Act. The act not only controlled the disposal of medical waste but also banned all ocean dumping of sewage sludge by 1992. *Sewage sludge* is a technical term, referring to the moist, dunglike residue of toxic chemicals, infectious agents and settled solids recovered at waste treatment plants or possibly at dockside restrooms. Waste not dumped into the ocean, however, must be dumped somewhere else. New York City now sends its treated sewage on a two-thousand-mile train ride to Texas. Many environmental laws don't so much solve a problem as transfer it.

Environmental laws? More than eleven hundred U.S. cities still lawfully discharge billions of gallons of raw sewage into estuaries and coastal waters. After extensive regulation and modest improvement, the Chesapeake Bay, a nearly closed system that takes in only about 1 percent of new water each year, might as well be a multistate toilet bowl. Despite all the environmental laws enacted since Congress passed the National Environmental Policy Act in 1969, the United States releases more than 3.5 billion pounds of toxic chemicals into the environment yearly. *Billion.* Not counting another 2 billion pounds of pesticides. Not counting the billions and billions of pounds produced by the rest of the industrial world. Much of this worldwide toxic fallout, of course, finds its way eventually into the ocean.

Then, too, legislation normally responds to existing damage, so it can't deal with dangers that for years escape detection, like the infamous hole in the Antarctic ozone layer, now some three times the size of the continental United States. Over the next few decades, the depletion of stratospheric ozone by manufactured chlorofluorocarbons (CFCs) promises to cause hundreds of thousands of human skin cancers. What harm will nonhuman life suffer, or what will the unknown consequences hold for us? Although UN members under the 1987 Montreal Protocol agreed to phase out CFC production by the year 2000, which is good news, the long-lasting damage will accelerate for at least another generation. Laws always lag behind our capacity to invent fresh abuses. The almost unregulated new field of biotechnology threatens to do for plant and animal life what the Industrial Revolution has done for the air and water.

Even good laws, though clearly needed, somehow miss the point. Laws tend to cast problems as violations "out there"—in the ozone layer, in the cities, in the oceans—an external danger we can control with external safeguards such as bureaucratic regulations, better enforcement, sunblock, floppy hats and new "safe" chemicals for our refrigerators and air conditioners. But suppose the problem is not so much external as internal? Not out there but in here? Not them but us? We resist this idea like poison.

One popular form of resistance is to blame environmentalists for stirring up trouble. But environmentalists also employ their own form of resistance, often shifting all the blame to industry. Capital-bashing and green-bashing, however, simply divide the world into good guys and bad guys—categories, like pronouns, that shift to fit everyone equally. Every talk show can drag out a zealot primed to attack environmentalists or to blast DuPont. No one in the history of TV or cinema *admits* to being the bad guy.

Here is the most troubling thought. Even if we as individuals could admit our role in damaging the planet, the admission would not be enough. Serious environmental damage to air, water and wildlife usually crosses state and national borders. Unfortunately we just don't have much experience in addressing interconnected regional and global problems to which real solutions, not merely shipping the sewage sludge somewhere else, may require us to question some of the deepest assumptions of Western culture. Will we be able to change? In time?

A short plane ride doesn't lend itself to solving the riddle of the sphinx. Still, as we touch down in San Jose, I feel something like a personal conviction growing within me. No one wants to hear it, but by simply going about our lives as 5.6 billion twentieth-century consumers, soon to double our numbers, we reconfigure the planet in irreversible ways that damage it forever.

My motives for seeking out Paul Watson, then, are both general, embracing large questions about our relationship to the earth, and personal. During the years I spent more or less asleep to environmental damage, pursuing an academic career and writing books, Paul Watson has been living on the edge, without much support or understanding, without safety nets, putting his life repeatedly at risk to protect endangered species. He sails his ships on a shoestring budget, with all-volunteer crews, far out into the open seas where pirate whalers and driftnet trawlers systematically pillage the ocean. When he catches up with them, he rams their ships, sinks their nets and puts them out of business. Paul Watson is a modern environmental Robin Hood with—not surprisingly—a price on his head.

Although he employs methods that his opponents label unethical or illegal, such methods might put him in the company of the patriots who dumped British tea into Boston Harbor. Significantly, though he has sometimes been arrested and charged, he has never been convicted of a crime. Often he asks—even demands—that the authorities arrest him, even traveling to Iceland in 1988 where he publicly claimed responsibility for sinking half the Icelandic whaling fleet. The governments and corporations he confronts, however, usually don't want their acts exposed to public scrutiny or discussion. The sole response from the government of Iceland was, illegally, to deport him.

From far off, Paul Watson seems an almost impossible figure: a cross between Saint Francis and Rambo. Even allies in the environmental movement sometimes denounce him in order to maintain a safe distance from his controversial tactics. Many of the denunciations boil down to little more than attacks on his character. He is called headstrong, polemical, combative, simplistic, meddlesome, arrogant. Maybe so. But that's only part of the story. And even if such attacks were entirely justified, they wouldn't call into question his commitment or his merit in defending the environment. Paul Watson is far more complicated than the stage villain his opponents choose to condemn.

Other attacks conceal a more indirect antagonism. Although some environmental groups reward their executives with lavish incomes and fat expense accounts, the tiny Sea Shepherd staff works mostly without a paycheck. Watson draws no salary. He supports himself solely by occasional lectures, writing and teaching. What he lacks in resources, however, he makes up for in boldness and dedication. His life has an authenticity that no organization can duplicate. He has slipped through FBI lines to help the embattled Sioux Indians at Wounded Knee. In protest against the annual slaughter of harp seal pups off Newfoundland, he has stood motionless while a huge icebreaker crashed toward him through the frozen sea.

"A crummy way to die," his shipmate Bob Hunter recalls him saying as they waited for the icebreaker to bury them.

The former Minister of the Environment for British Columbia, Rafe Mair, writes simply, "Paul Watson is the most courageous man I have ever known."

There isn't really a category elastic enough to fit him. The term he prefers, alluding to the ancient Samurai swordsmen who lived by a strict code of harmony with nature, is "Earth Warrior."

No one would confuse me with a Samurai warrior. I'm mostly nonconfrontational, mild if occasionally stubborn, and I don't like codes. The sea appeals to me mainly as a spectacle. Swimming and boating I avoid whenever possible, despite a nautical ancestry. Two of my great grandfathers captained high-masted schooners out of Nova Scotia, and my grandfather ran a maritime shipping agency, but somehow the saltwater genes slipped right past me.

Yet, no matter how much I feel, by comparison, like the high-seas version of Samurai Chicken, I also know I *must* come along on this campaign. I will be sailing not as an environmentalist and not as an activist—certainly not as an adventurer—but as a forty-nine-year-old writer who believes that Paul Watson ranks among the most extraordinary individuals of our time. What is he like? What does he think? What drives him to risk his life for a handful of apparently doomed marine species? What, if anything, does he have to teach us? The search for answers is at least as compelling, for me, as the search for driftnet ships.

⚓ ⚓ ⚓

The plane ride, with almost too much leisure for thought, has left me feeling a little apprehensive as I walk through the San Jose airport to catch a shuttle van to Santa Cruz. I miss Ruth already, and after a week on the road, the prospect of an open-ended voyage into the North Pacific to ram a ship and maybe get killed doesn't exactly set my mind at ease. What I need, desperately, is a good omen. As I approach the shuttle kiosk, I notice a woman sitting hunched over, inhaling a cigarette with great concentration. As she turns slightly to one side, I recognize her as my old friend Valerie Lagorio, professor of medieval literature at the University of Iowa and an international authority on fourteenth-century women mystics. Omen supplied.

I haven't seen Valerie since we taught together over a decade ago, and we jabber away during the ride to Santa Cruz like army buddies reunited after the war. The talk helps restore a sense that I am not just walking off into the void. There is no way, however, to avoid explaining why I just happened to turn up at a kiosk several thousand miles from my home in Michigan. I improvise a few sketchy comments about Paul Watson and his penchant for ramming ships.

The *Sea Shepherd II* at anchor in Monterey Bay

Valerie leans over and listens carefully. As the van arrives at her stop in Santa Cruz, she puts her hand on my arm and in a serious tone says, "I'll pray for you."

If anyone could get a prayer through on my behalf, given my doubts about organized religion, it would be Valerie. Maybe she could ask one of her sainted fourteenth-century mystics to intercede, like Catherine of Siena, who composed probably the most daring book ever written: her main character, speaking almost incessantly for three hundred pages, is God. With Valerie gone and Saint Catherine a doubtful ally, the ride to the highway motel leaves me once again on my own. Another long, restless night.

Sunday morning finds me standing on the Santa Cruz municipal wharf at 10:00, bags in hand, gazing out at Monterey Bay, where about a half-mile distant the *Sea Shepherd II*—an imposing silhouette—rides serenely at anchor.

CHAPTER TWO

PROTEUS RISING

• • •

Some steps, we know without being told, are big ones, like getting married or leaping off the top of a tall building. They exude an air of seriousness, if not finality. In a way that distinguishes them from all other actions, they are profoundly irreversible. They also contain a powerful element of the unknown and the unknowable. Luckily, there is no one to watch me fret in my Santa Cruz motel room early Sunday morning as I spend a final hour writing brief good-bye letters to Ruth, to our daughter, Ellen, and to my parents.

My fairly well-armed common sense tries to stand guard against creeping melodrama, shutting down the recurrent visions of my legs being torn off by sharks, but as I write, I also know that I might *not* come back. So there is a need to say things I wouldn't want to leave unsaid. Ramming ships and seizing driftnets mean danger—I can't possibly know how *much* danger—and my mind plays over the algebra of doubt, unable to leave it alone. Fresh reinforcements of common sense sweep in to remind me that Watson insists his Sea Shepherd campaigns, however risky, have never injured anyone. Still, there's always a first time. In July 1986, the Faeroe Islands police used rifle fire and tear gas against the *Sea Shepherd* crew.

Perhaps everyone has a secret list of preferred ways not to die. Gnawed by rats, buried alive, boiled in oil: a very personal horror story deposited deep in the primal psyche. Death at sea has always struck me as absolutely the worst way to go. My archetypal nightmare is the scene from *Moby Dick* when Pip, the little black cook's assistant, a harmless landlubber, accidentally falls overboard as the *Pequod* sails on, leaving him alone at the center of the expanding empty circle of the horizon. He dies a madman.

Fortunately, I have a number of last-minute details to occupy me before the taxi arrives. With most of my clothes sealed in the depths of the U.S. Postal Service, I have kept only two pairs of jeans, some underwear and a few T-shirts. After a final check of the motel room, including a fast tour through the heirloom leather gym bag holding my most precious new acquisitions—the tape recorder, camera and five lab books—I grab my wristwatch from the nightstand and start for the door. Strangely, I can't remember which wrist to put the watch on. It feels uncomfortable either way.

I drop the wristwatch deep into the gym bag as if to the bottom of the sea and pull the zipper shut.

⚓ ⚓ ⚓

The taxi, a vehicle so damaged it could advertise as a bad omen, takes me to the Santa Cruz municipal wharf. The wharf juts far out into the bay, lined with shops and benches, and a glance into one of the shop windows assures me that I'm on time. At this early hour on Sunday morning only a few stray fishermen and tourists are out. A feeling of relief surges through me again as I gaze at the *Sea Shepherd II* about a half mile offshore. There's only one problem: I have no idea how to get onboard. I wave my white Huskies cap above my head in wide arcs, but after minutes of waving I conclude that my signal is apparently unnoticed or indecipherable.

Where is Paul Watson? I put the cap back on and look around, wondering what to do next. One self-protective layer of neocortex secretly cheers that maybe I won't have to go. Then I recall, with a rush of shame, that I was once too reckless for such—what's the word I want—irresolution?

So, I stroll along the sidewalk, past the few scattered fishermen who peer over the rail at their lines piercing the dark grey surface fifty or sixty feet below. This is crazy. Stepping carefully so as not to slam the fishermen with my gear, I try a lot of hanging around, more hat waving, shift to different locations. Sometimes, while I wave my hat, with the other hand I lift my sleeping bag shoulder high. The message seems clear enough to me. But maybe from out in the bay I look like a demented tourist making obscure gestures with his luggage toward the Pacific Ocean.

After some time, I suddenly notice a small, faded rubber dinghy puttering drowsily toward the wharf, headed apparently for a water-level platform where the parasail concession launches its rides. I hadn't noticed the platform before, maybe because a chain bearing a "Closed" sign blocked off the steep wooden stairs leading down from the wharf. The dinghy looks so beat-up and aimless that I start to turn away. But something strikes me as odd, so I look more closely at the figure by the outboard motor, who from my post high on the wharf resembles a lean, tan beachcomber in baggy shorts. As he pulls closer, I can make out dim block letters on the dinghy: *Sea Shepherd II.*

Surprise number one: the beachcomber turns out to be Jon Huntemer, captain (pro tem) of the *Sea Shepherd II.* Surprise two: he knows nothing about picking me up. Paul, I learn, hasn't arrived and hasn't sent word about our 10:00 appointment. Jon has docked at the parasail platform with the sole purpose of picking up several crew members, who didn't show. When I tell him about my agreement to meet Paul, Jon shrugs as if things like this happen all the time. I begin to sense that arrangements in the Sea Shepherd Conservation Society have a slightly improvisational feel. Or maybe it's more like loosely orchestrated chaos. In any case, it's not reassuring.

Jon, despite his captain's rank, hasn't shaved in several days. I pass my duffel down into the wobbling dinghy—Jon calls it a "zodiac"—and hunker atop my new sleeping bag, holding on tight to a thin rope behind me, secured God only knows where, as we putter off toward the big black ship waiting solemnly out in Monterey Bay.

The *Sea Shepherd II* appears to grow larger and larger as we approach until, with the gnatlike zodiac tied up alongside, I feel the full impact of its looming 189-foot length. It looks graceful from a distance, a high pointed bow sloping to a low, wide middle, then gradually rising and narrowing toward the stern. Climbing up the slippery wooden rungs of the rope ladder—it seems like scaling a mountain—I notice a crudely patched hole in the hull, about the dimensions of a medium-size television set, and a lot of rust. Jon tells me that Canada impounded the ship for two years and left it to rot. They didn't even drain the seawater from the pipes, which effectively corroded the engine-cooling system. This information does not increase my confidence, and I turn my eyes away from the patch.

What puzzles me as I swing firmly onto the thick planks of the deck is a list of odd names in white block letters along the

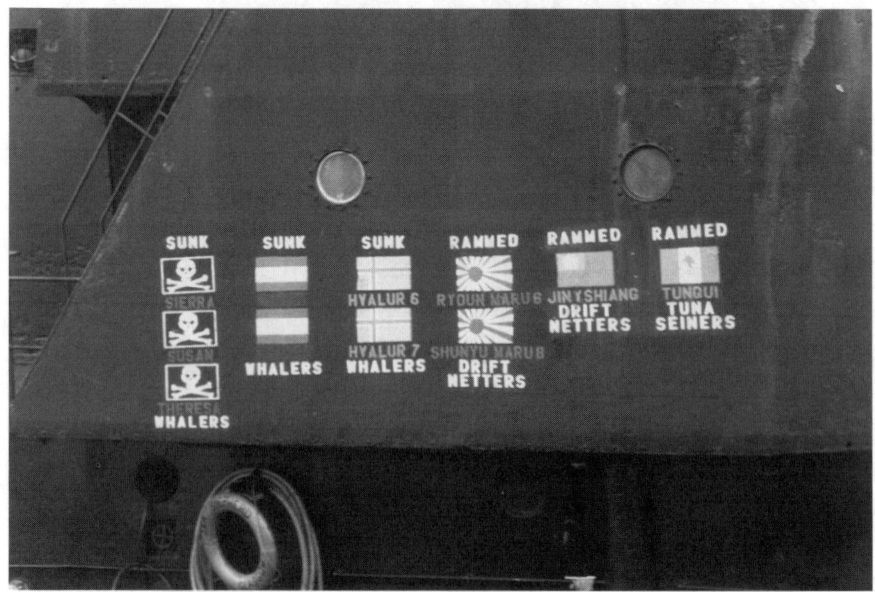

The names of rammed or sunk ships are painted on the *Sea Shepherd II*.

side of the bridge, just beneath a painted skull and crossbones. Then, suddenly, it makes sense. Each name identifies a ship that Paul has sunk or otherwise put out of commission. The *Sea Shepherd II* carries its history emblazoned on its side like notches in a six-gun. Even the Roman numeral *II* conveys a sense of tradition that links the rusting black trawler with its sister ship, the original *Sea Shepherd,* and with the most notorious name stenciled on its side: the pirate whaler *Sierra.*

⚓ ⚓ ⚓

The *Sierra* had a well-deserved reputation as the most infamous pirate ship of modern times, and for years Paul had hoped to find and destroy it. The *Sierra* hunted whales, and had done so continuously since 1960, at first in the Antarctic (until the blue whale population collapsed) and later off Angola and the coast of Africa. Every week it destroyed another ten whales, day in, day out, including mothers, infants and endangered species.

Like most whalers, the *Sierra* initially worked together with a factory ship that processed the meat, but in the late 1960s the Dutch owners converted the *Sierra* into an all-purpose industrial mill that hunted the whales, slaughtered them and stored the quick-frozen meat for transfer to cargo vessels. Subsequent owners—Norwegian banks and a Japanese corporation—hid their identities through a carefully constructed screen of international businesses, which included a South African whaling company. Without question, however, the whale meat headed ultimately to Japan.

This superefficient killing machine crisscrossed the seas for two decades with its harpoon cannon on the bow and a slanted rear deck where chains dragged the whale carcasses directly into the bowels of the foul-smelling ship to be cut up into steaks by Japanese butchers. It was a hideous, floating, nonstop production line that might still be operating today if not for Paul Watson.

How do you catch an outlaw ship? You buy a ship of your own and start hunting. In 1978, with $120,000 supplied by

Cleveland Amory, president of the Fund for Animals, Paul purchased a nineteen-year-old, retired British cod trawler that he renamed the *Sea Shepherd*. It was no beauty. Covered with grotesque yellow paint, rusting, idle since Britain ended its cod war with Iceland, on first inspection the ship seemed to Paul, as he put it, "a scabrous, dying thing." He also suspected that, once sandblasted, the three-inch-thick steel hull would reveal pure, unpitted metal. Sure enough. Painted battleship grey, reinforced with eighteen tons of concrete in its bow, the *Sea Shepherd* emerged as a taut, menacing predator ready to take on even such elusive giants as the *Sierra*.

Its first campaign in March 1979 took the *Sea Shepherd* to the ice-bound Gulf of St. Lawrence off Newfoundland, near the Magdalen Islands, where Paul led his third expedition to disrupt the annual hunt of harp seal pups. *Hunt,* of course, is a euphemism, since the pups made no effort to escape. The sealer simply walked up to the white-furred newborn harp seals, bashed their heads in and skinned them on the spot, sometimes leaving them still twitching on bloodstained ice.

Paul's plan—to spray the pups with bright red dye to make their pelts commercially useless—did not sit well with the Canadian Fisheries Ministry, the Quebec Provincial Police or the Royal Canadian Mounted Police. The slaughter of harp seal pups was a local tradition and big business. Fur coats for sale abroad made a few Canadian families immensely rich. Paul, for his troubles, was arrested, beaten unconscious and later escaped with just seconds to spare from an enraged mob. He had experienced such responses before.

Cleveland Amory didn't think that Paul, even fully recovered, stood a chance of finding the *Sierra*. Locating a single ship somewhere off the coast of Europe, Africa or South America, without a clue as to where or how to start, had about the same likelihood of success as saying "Please stop" to a harp seal hunter. Undeterred, Paul persuaded Amory to give him one month to find the *Sierra* before they turned to less improbable targets.

Four months later off the coast of Portugal, in mid-July 1979, Paul, to his astonishment, finally caught sight of the *Sierra*. He had no experience in ramming ships—he even lugged mattresses onto the bridge to cushion the expected blow—but he knew he couldn't let the *Sierra* escape. He figured that hitting the *Sierra* while still on the high seas could injure its crew, so he decided to follow it into port, in Leixoes, and ram it against the concrete wharves. It was a good plan, mostly, except that the Portuguese authorities conspired to let the *Sierra* slip out of port while entangling Paul in bureaucratic red tape and refusing him permission to depart.

Paul knew that to disobey the authorities and pursue the *Sierra* might earn everyone on his ship long sentences in a Portuguese jail. He explained the dangers, offering crew members several minutes to decide whether to join him. All but two of the sixteen crew members elected to leave the ship. Joined only by chief engineer Peter Woolf and third engineer Jerry Doran, Paul then steered the *Sea Shepherd* out of Leixoes harbor, with no pilot, no clearance and in absolute defiance of Portuguese law. The captain of the *Sierra* assumed that only a madman would leave port without authorization, so Paul caught up with him easily as the ship idled just outside Leixoes harbor. Paul and his two-man skeleton crew fired up their engines and aimed the *Sea Shepherd* like a battering ram.

The first blow glanced slightly, but the second cut a huge, forty-foot gash in the hull of the *Sierra*. They could even see the whale meat hanging inside.

Before they could launch a third and final blow, sending it to the bottom, the *Sierra* started its engines and headed back for the harbor. The Portuguese, meanwhile, sent a warship in pursuit of the *Sea Shepherd*, which was caught and impounded. They eventually let Paul leave the country, informing him after many delays that it would cost

$750,000 in fines and damages to regain possession of the *Sea Shepherd*. Otherwise the ship would be turned over to the owners of the *Sierra*. The ransom—no other word quite applies—was ridiculous. The *Sea Shepherd* had cost far less to buy, and Paul could not tolerate letting his ship revert to the outlaw owners of the *Sierra*.

Only one choice remained. Paul returned to Portugal along with Peter Woolf, who flew back from Australia. On inspection, he and Peter discovered that the *Sea Shepherd* was being looted for spare parts while the Portuguese impounded it. They had no hope of stealing back the disabled ship or of eluding the Portuguese navy. Secretly, in the darkness of New Year's Eve 1979, Paul stood guard as Peter Woolf unscrewed a crucial plate in the engine room, slowly but inexorably flooding the *Sea Shepherd* and sinking it to the bottom of shallow Leixoes harbor.

The next morning Paul returned—a dangerous move as the docks now swarmed with rifle-carrying soldiers—and saw his beloved, valiant ship half-submerged, its bow pointing skyward. Hastily he and Peter Woolf split up, escaping from Portugal as fugitives.

A little over one month later in a Quebec courtroom, on trial for his earlier violation of the Canadian Seal Protection Act, Paul received a telephone call. The informant told him that three environmentalists in wet suits, carrying magnetic explosive mines, had just slipped into Lisbon harbor and blown up the *Sierra*. Within ten minutes it turned over and sank. Another caller told the press they did it for the *Sea Shepherd*.

⚓ ⚓ ⚓

Walking the rough plank deck of the *Sea Shepherd II*, which replaced its scuttled namesake in November 1980, I feel enfolded into a history unknown to the spectators who buzz the mysterious black ship in their fiberglass cabin cruisers and sailboats. Probably few crew members know that back in 1980, in a stroke of cash poetry, Paul bought the *Sea Shepherd II* with money he received from Warner Brothers for movie rights to the *Sierra* campaign. Whatever their status as historians, crew members of the *Sea Shepherd II* don't mind giving informal tours to sightseers, and right now four men who look like middle-aged executives are touring the bow. Sporting pastel polo shirts and deck shoes, they've sailed down from San Francisco for a long weekend. One holds the *Sea Shepherd II* flag out straight so his pal can snap a photo: a white skull above a crossed tomahawk and shepherd's crook, on a field of sable. From the bridge I gaze back toward the wharf and see the spot where I stood three hours ago waving my cap. The fishermen at the rail are barely visible.

Jon assigns me a lower bunk in a dark, compact room off a dark, narrow corridor somewhere far below deck. The bunk, a slab of bare plywood, at least makes a good surface to write on, if only I could see my pen. Aha! I congratulate myself on bringing a flashlight. Jon, meanwhile, disappears, so I shoot a beam around the warren of rough wooden bunkbeds. To judge by the absence of bags, I'm the only person assigned here. In the darkness, recalling the multilevel network of ladders and dim corridors, I wonder if I'll

The *Sea Shepherd II* flag: a shepherd's crook, a trident and a skull

ever find my way back. The feeling of being surrounded—or engulfed—by substandard equipment has been growing steadily.

Fortunately Jon returns and shows me through the ship—galley, engine room, head—and then, with turns and detours impossible to retrace, we climb three or four staircases to the bridge. The surprises continue. On the bridge a big, handsome, scruffily dressed crew member in a black baseball cap stained even blacker immediately shouts hello. Someone here knows me? Sure enough, it's Sam. Nobody uses Sam's given name, John Barwick, just as nobody on the *Sea Shepherd II* uses last names at all. Only a glance at the captain's log reveals that Scamp's mother once gave him the perfectly respectable name George Moulton.

Sam and I met once in Key West, and he's pretty hard to forget with his scraggly beard, friendly smile and teeth so strong they look borrowed from a statue. He also seems to be wearing the very same shorts and cap he wore in Key West. His grease-soaked clothes must hold the world record for oil-to-fiber ratio. Sam's tan, muscular body is a reminder that clean clothing can be overrated. He exudes a healthy outdoors brawn that gym rats pumped up on steroids and chrome dumbbells just can't reproduce.

It must be a somewhat unusual bridge. I notice on the broad flat surface beyond the wheel, like the dashboard of a car except enlarged to ship size, a copy of John Muir's *Wilderness Essays*. A week-old *USA Today* and an open twelve-pack of Hamm's beer lie discarded in a corner. The crew have been living on the ship for more than a month, working on repairs here in Santa Cruz, with a little time left over to explore the local bars. Apparently the people in Santa Cruz like them. Sam says the crew has a hard time finding a bar where they aren't treated to free drinks. Nothing more will happen until Paul Watson arrives from Long Beach on the *Edward Abbey*. But, as I've learned the hard way, Paul is not here yet.

Someone shouts, "Food's ready!"

What kind of cuisine is served on the *Sea Shepherd II*? Pasta. Pasta, salad, beans and rice. No meat. The cook, a bespectacled, scholarly-looking man around forty, listens to my story about a last-minute decision to join the ship and then tops it. A former L.A. executive with a chain of five stores based on trendy Rodeo Drive, he has recently finished his first year of law school. His name is Stuart Steele. Speaking with a soft accent that evokes southern roots, he says quietly that he needed to change his life and do something positive for the environment. So a week ago he signed on as cook.

The pasta is first-rate. I eat it leaning against a metal pole surrounded by a melee of hanging pots and kitchen implements as we continue our conversation. Stuart says he wants to use his executive experience and legal training to set up an institute for funding innovative programs in environmental protection. Not your ordinary cook, but he's not atypical here. Several women have joined up, one supposedly the daughter of a well-known Latin American finance minister. Overall, the crew of the *Sea Shepherd II* is a UN of unique and unusual people: British, Danish, Mexican, Australian, Peruvian, American. Paul, of course, is Canadian.

After lunch I spend a few hours on deck adjusting to the gentle roll of the bay and trying out the inscrutable electronic menu on my new camera. Then, through trial and mostly error, I make my way back to my cabin to change film. The room resembles a dimly lit tomb. Then, with a loud shudder, like an enormous furnace shutting down, the lights go out and I'm standing in blind total darkness. Power failure.

Power failures, I learn, happen regularly on the *Sea Shepherd II*. Shifting position in the dark, I feel a sharp sting on the back of my lower leg. I freeze on instinct. I grope for my flashlight and shine it toward the area where I hope to find the source of my pain. Expecting maybe a rat or a snake, I'm relieved that nothing seems unusual, no paws or scrabbling sounds. At last the flashlight picks out a shiny, sturdy nail protruding, point-first, from the opposite bunk.

Jesus! What idiot would leave a nail sticking out! The word *tetanus* flashes through my mind. Yes, I'm a little jumpy. This is not the secure, finish-carpentered world I'm used to. But the same middle-class impulse that made me buy a flashlight also suggested a first-aid kit, which I exhume like buried treasure from my leather gym bag. Aiming the flashlight dead ahead, I cautiously work my way back to the galley looking for water to wash out the puncture wound.

Stuart tells me there's no distilled water left. In the light from a nearby porthole, the pale brown liquid dribbling out of the ship's tap looks like a menagerie of bacteria. A young woman, perhaps sensing the panic beneath my barely controlled calm, takes a teakettle from the stove and pours warm water onto the threadbare washcloth I liberated this morning from the overpriced Santa Cruz motel. I remember that before leaving the motel I swallowed the last tablet in a two-week course of antibiotics, which cheers me up a little, figuring that my blood is potent enough to kill vampires. *Killer blood.* The phrase soothes me, and I repeat it like a mantra as I carefully tend my wound. Smoothing on antibiotic cream, I apply a bandage and realize there's nothing more I can do. The flashlight beam makes the darkness more oppressive, so I opt to thread the maze of ladders up to daylight.

My mood improves up on deck. The sun and water and the lush California coastline impart peacefulness. Then, too, there are surprises to discover in odd corners of the ship. Unfortunately, the ship looks worse the closer I examine it—a primitive, diesel-powered campsite.

The engines chug on, sounding more confident, and I'm caught in a sudden backdraft of thick blue smoke.

⚓ ⚓ ⚓

God, I'm depressed! What am I doing here? I just made a quick trip to the wharf via the zodiac and called Ruth from an outdoor phone adjacent to the public restrooms. Some setting for good-byes. Various crew members claim that Paul and the *Edward Abbey* are just a few hours out of Santa Cruz. Meanwhile Jon holds long, tense discussions with an electrician. As they confer, chief engineer David Cole and his two whiz-kid assistants, Myra Finkelstein and Sue Rodriguez-Pastor, lean in. David Cole is so quiet and slight that he seems almost invisible, except for shorts encrusted with enough engine grime to show up on radar. He previously worked as a bicycle mechanic. Bearded, intense, he mulls over the electrical problems with total absorption.

One of the alternators is bad. How do we get current to the ship's exterior lights? Will the DC generator charge the AC generator upstairs? Jon follows the responses with the eyes of a captain who knows he can't afford to be fifteen hundred miles from land with no power.

The *Sea Shepherd II*, I'm learning, is a steel derelict. Its inner organs are shot, rust peels from the girders in bold orange sheets and something is always going wrong.

I notice that the average age of the crew must be about twenty. The ship has the air of a children's crusade. Mark Heitchue, the skinny, redheaded boatswain temporarily second in command, passed me at the wharf on his way to mail in his senior thesis. (College, not high school. I checked.) Chris Maenz, one of the women struggling to repair the ship's lights, graduated just this spring from the University of Montana. I don't mean to knock education—or youth. Still, a tad more age and experience among my crewmates isn't such a terrible wish, is it? I must be the oldest person on board.

God, I'm depressed.

⚓ ⚓ ⚓

It is a couple of hours before midnight as I sit alone on the high bow of the *Sea Shepherd II* repeating the words "Killer Blood." There's no one in sight. Right now I don't care if we all have to pack up and go home. A few scattered exterior bulbs lend the deserted, corroded, shadow-black deck an impression of impending doom. I almost expect to hear a scream or gunshot. Suddenly a single blinding light, like the headlamp of a locomotive, looms out of the darkness. As the light moves steadily closer, I hear what sounds like clanking metal and I wheel around in barely controlled panic, feeling doubly deserted. In the eerie nighttime surroundings I wonder momentarily if I've been singled out for abduction by a spaceship. Then, with a nimble slide, the *Edward Abbey* circles round the bow and skids to a halt some two hundred feet away. Paul Watson has arrived.

The appearance of Paul Watson functions like a factory whistle. People shoot out from nowhere and plunge into a frenzy of continuous labor. I, too, put in long hours—as a deckhand—after a precarious midnight zodiac ride transfers me to the *Edward Abbey*. In my first job, I help pump out a spare fuel tank that has sprung a pinhole leak on the run from Santa Cruz. The tank, located directly underneath the crew's quarters, fills the cramped cabin above with the stink of diesel fumes. We race for every fire extinguisher on board as Scamp lowers a large fan down the hatch for ventilation and slowly begins pumping out the flammable bilge.

Later a young crew member in a ponytail, Ken Walker, enlists my help carrying a fifty-gallon oil drum—some four hundred pounds of sloshing liquid—along the narrow, slippery metal deck from bow to stern. Somehow we manage to lift it over a knee-high pipe that blocks our way. This is no time to think about the bad back I've been nursing up the coast. The work goes on all night, and I finally collapse into my bunk about dawn.

After a few hours of sleep the work starts again. I'm pressed into service unloading the two zodiacs as they zip all day between the *Sea Shepherd II* and the *Edward Abbey*, transferring food, crew and supplies. A chaos of fruit and vegetables spills across the deck in an overflow of massive floppy cardboard boxes, but no one has said anything about meals, and I don't ask. Nearly dazed with hunger, in the vacant galley I find two cold, leftover muffins on the griddle—their bottoms slick with grease—and stuff them down my throat fast, like a thief.

We're supposed to depart this afternoon, but the automatic pilot on the *Edward Abbey* has broken, and Scamp just left for the marina to get it fixed. The friendly, talkative chief engineer I met in San Pedro has turned into a glowering thug. Last night the leaking fuel tank put him in a foul temper. Earlier today I heard him tell Jim Knapp, who works with Ken in the engine room, that the *Edward Abbey* should be put in dry dock and have its entire hull checked with ultrasound. Jim, a shipyard welder, has complained to Scamp about a faulty weld on the hull below the waterline where he can't repair it. Rumors are flying.

The *Edward Abbey*, though much smaller at a mere ninety-five feet and much less stable with its flat bottom and shallow keel, has two advantages over the *Sea Shepherd II:* it's newer and faster. I'm not convinced it's in much better shape. A large rat trap set with a ball of coagulated fat rests near the stairs leading down from the deck to the galley. The tiny cabin I share with Meg Larsen has no ventilation and no natural light. With the door closed, it could be midnight on the moon.

It surprised me to find myself assigned to share a cabin with a woman. Meg is a schoolteacher in her late twenties from outside Detroit, with short brown hair and the long legs of a sprinter. She turns out to be Beth's younger sister, feisty and opinionated, unfazed by tough conditions, a down-to-earth, no-nonsense "girl next door." I come to like the idea that Meg and I have been thrown together in this windowless box. Some critics describe the environmental movement as the last all-male club—clearly they know nothing about ecofeminism—but the Sea Shepherd Conservation Society has no evident gender bias. Meg and Chris Maenz give the nine-member *Edward Abbey* crew a strong female presence.

Troubling signs continue to appear. On the bridge, tending the radio while Scamp checks out a faulty steering motor, I see a sturdy baseball bat half-hidden in one corner. A baseball bat? A little later my eye catches two military helmets and two heavy plates of body armor below the four-step metal staircase leading from the bridge to the radio room. In an almost conspiratorial tone, Scamp grumbles about a stress fracture. In calm seas it shouldn't matter, he says. In high seas, the pounding of thirty- to fifty-foot waves could be fatal.

There's trouble between Scamp and Jim. I can't get to the bottom of it, but Jim clearly feels unappreciated. With his wiry build, black hair, pale skin and permanent dark glasses, he looks more like a jazz musician than an unemployed welder. In fact he quit the only regular job he'd held in two years to join this campaign. That's dedication, foolishness or an entirely un-American attitude toward paid labor. He seems high-strung and a bit difficult, but he's also burned-out from weeks of unremitting hard work. His voice sounds too calm, as if straining to hold back a flood of emotion. Scamp has run out of patience with him: "I got no time for his personal problems." Something seems about to break.

⚓ ⚓ ⚓

Departures are rarely clean-cut affairs, but I doubt that Paul will delay our exit and put the *Edward Abbey* into dry dock. Last night I saw him just once, despite the press of crew members at work, and today, too, he has been mostly out of sight. Now he looks ready and determined. In an open blouse, wearing a thick black belt and large brass buckle with "Sea Shepherd" in raised block script, he looks like a pirate with a weakness for good causes. He clearly feels at home. I, by contrast, am in every sense at sea.

Paul radios the *Sea Shepherd II* with the news that we embark at 7:30 tonight. Mist and rain have moved in, and the water has turned quite choppy. Too choppy, in fact, to bring the *Edward Abbey* alongside the *Sea Shepherd II* so they can process our bilgewater in their oil/water separator. It's illegal to dump bilgewater containing waste oil, so the oil must be separated and stored, but of course our oil/water separator is broken. On the bridge Paul says his good-byes to Beth. (Are they lovers?) Meanwhile the sea has become so rough that the *Edward Abbey* pitches helplessly from side to side. Beth, perky almost to the last, slips and badly injures her knee as she climbs down the rope ladder into the zodiac bobbing crazily beside the pitching ship. Her ride to shore can't be pleasant. So long, darlin'.

As the winds rise further and darkness falls, Paul sits alone on the bridge blowing into a large conch shell, like an ancient Hebrew forcing music from a ram's horn shofar. It's an unearthly sound, perhaps his way of signaling the start of a campaign—a call to battle—or making contact with the spirit of the sea. I think of Wordsworth's great sonnet that begins "The world is too much with us"—about how we waste our powers in the daily grind of earning a livelihood, out of tune with nature, forsaken, unfeeling. Wordsworth ends by saying that he'd rather be an ancient pagan bred on falsehoods, if only he could feel the presence of supernatural forces moving through the world and glimpse again the lost gods of nature:

> Have sight of Proteus rising from the sea;
> Or hear old Triton blow his wreathed horn.

Proteus: Greek shape-shifter, the original Old Man of the Sea, shepherd to the oceanic flocks. Something very pagan and primal is happening here. If the night gets any wilder, we will do some serious rocking and rolling.

CHAPTER THREE

FEDS

• • •

Just moments before our scheduled departure last night, the *Sea Shepherd II* received a message over the ship's radio to "stand by." We would be boarded and searched by a party of agents from the U.S. Customs Service. It wasn't a request but an order—and at a very strange time. The agents lingered on board for quite a while with the wind increasing its howl. Like Beth, on leaving they almost lost their footing as they grappled, in near-darkness, with the flailing rope ladder that flapped several feet above their wildly tossing zodiac. Unfortunately I missed most of the action because I stayed below deck with an advanced case of seasickness.

⚓ ⚓ ⚓

Paul, in his last-minute arrangements, decided to shanghai Stuart Steele to fill out the *Edward Abbey* crew. The addition of Stuart as cook is good news, as I liked him immediately when we talked the other day in the galley. Apparently the young woman I met in San Pedro, who described herself as the cook, couldn't cook a lick, so she and her silent boyfriend were left behind—*fired* is the term I hear—leaving the *Edward Abbey* in urgent need of someone who knows how to boil potatoes. Enter Stuart, who doesn't hide his regrets about leaving the friends he made aboard the *Sea Shepherd II*. It's lucky for us he's so flexible and good-natured because the scene awaiting him in the galley looks like bomb damage.

Stuart Steele in the ship's galley

Stuart and I, despite the press of work, took a few minutes to chat on deck before the mist and rain descended yesterday. He was reflecting on the young crew—most between seventeen and twenty-three—who have slaved for weeks preparing the two ships for departure. Among the details he recounted about his varied careers, Stuart mentioned that he spent several years in Texas supervising a restaurant, where he discovered that his employees had no interest in hard work. He survived by learning to expect only what they were prepared to give. This young crew, by contrast, labor almost nonstop. They may joke a bit and banter on the job, but they keep toiling long after paid workers would have punched the clock and disappeared. Stuart sees their energy and seriousness as coming from sheer commitment to the environment.

A similar commitment seemed obvious to me among the students who enrolled for a college course I taught just a few months ago during a ten-week stint as visiting fireman. Their main question about the environmental damage they saw all around them was simple: what could they do? Is dormitory recycling really an effective response to pollution, habitat destruction, industrial development and an exploding world population? Does it make any difference at all if you ride a bicycle rather than drive a car? The scruffy-looking young crew of the *Sea Shepherd II* obviously replies to such questions with action: herculean labor spent fixing up two old ships that should have been cut into scrap metal years ago. That's *before* they get to risk their lives a thousand miles at sea.

"It could be one of our more exciting trips," Paul told me as we parted in Long Beach. "I may sink the *Sea Shepherd II*."

There was no opportunity to ask how or why. I doubt Paul would have provided details. But of course he has a history of sinking ships, including his own. Scattered comments from crewmates suggest that we might expose the *Sea Shepherd II* to extensive damage in ramming driftnet ships and deliberately let it sink to the bottom on the voyage home. Cameras rolling. The film would capture a dramatic end for a ship that fought valiantly in a long, losing struggle to protect the environment. The plan, it seems to me, if that *was* the plan, has a few obvious holes.

⚓ ⚓ ⚓

I'm not depressed now. I'm sick. Seasick—elemental and absolute. Dog-sick. Last night I dreamed I was floating near the ceiling of a large room with a party going on underneath me as I passed over the heads of the guests. Awakening in my bunk, I discovered that with each movement of the ship I was pitching and rolling on the thin slab of foam rubber that serves as a mattress, my face and neck slick with sweat. My body keeps begging "Stop, stop!" but there's no stopping, nowhere to go, no time-outs. The rocking and pounding continue incessantly, amplified by the deep throbbing roar of the twin engines. Even moving my pen over the paper takes concentration, as does walking on the pitching metal deck that keeps slipping away beneath my feet. Nothing easy is easy anymore.

What's worst about the nausea is that I can't eat, can't keep food down and I'm beginning to feel dehydrated. Not even terminal thirst could force me to drink the brackish stuff that seeps out of the tap. If I don't keep something down soon, I'll be in trouble.

Meanwhile I've popped four Dramamine tablets after losing my breakfast this morning (a few crackers and a chunk of banana). The relief felt almost sensuous as I pressed my face against the cold metal pylon, mouth open, leaning past the single strand of wire that separates the deck from the sea. I'm not the only person aboard to race for the pylon. It seems far too early to deplete my wardrobe, but a change of clothes may boost my morale, and perhaps a little journal writing will help, too.

⚓ ⚓ ⚓

God knows what got me out of bed at 7:30 this morning. Still dazed and unsteady, I climb the steep metal ladder from the crew quarters to the small radio room, then weave up the four stairs from the radio room to the bridge. Staring in disbelief, I see the massive looming stern of the *Sea Shepherd II* less than twenty-five feet ahead. The *Edward Abbey* is closing fast, with Scamp and Chris near the bow, perilously bent over the single restraining wire as they struggle with a coil of thick rope. The seas look wild, and the bow of the *Edward Abbey* recklessly slams through the spray, now just fifteen feet or so from the mountainous rising and plunging stern of the *Sea Shepherd II*.

Paul, alone on the bridge, gazes ahead intently, left hand on the waist-high vertical wheel, right hand straddling the two levers that control our speed. He is barefoot, feet planted wide apart to brace himself against the violent side-to-side roll of the ship. The *Edward Abbey*—doubly pounded by the high seas and the wake of the *Sea Shepherd II*—now closes the distance to just a few yards. Paul wants to bring the two ships so close together that the *Sea Shepherd II* can toss us a towline. A sharp, quick spin of the wheel is sometimes all that keeps us from crashing head-on into the huge stern.

An almost surreal drama unfolds as the two plunging ships move toward a collision. The *Sea Shepherd II* rides so high, especially when a wave drops the *Edward Abbey* even lower than usual, that we seem about to be crushed like a speedboat beneath a freighter. Scamp and Chris—difficult to tell apart in the spray—lean far over the side trying to snag the towrope which, once attached, begins to billow out toward our propeller, where it could cause major damage. I serve as emergency conduit, stepping outside the bridge to shout messages from Paul, and finally, somehow, the job gets done. The towrope, half-floating on the waves, begins to tighten in a ragged arc connecting us like an umbilicus to the mother ship. Suddenly the rope lifts straight out of the water and stretches taut. Paul kills the engines.

A surge of relief temporarily erases my nausea. I make an inane but heartfelt remark in praise of Scamp and Chris who, soaked, exhausted and exultant, are raising their fists toward the bridge in victory.

"They're like twins," says Paul.

⚓ ⚓ ⚓

The talk on the bridge concerns our visit by the customs agent last night. The *Sea Shepherd II* is registered out of Glasgow and is thus not normally subject to U.S. Customs, but normal immunity vanishes in American waters. A Harbor Patrol zodiac hovered protectively nearby, bucking the heavy swells, apparently watching to make sure everything went by the book. The book, in this case, means routine paperwork concerning the ship's manifest, crew and cargo. It was a weird time for a routine check, however, especially considering the darkness and choppy seas. Obviously the customs agents had been monitoring radio communications between the *Edward Abbey* and the *Sea Shepherd II*, which explains how they learned the exact time of departure. Suddenly Paul understood why they had come.

"They're looking for Rod Coronado."

Rod Coronado, a legendary if shadowy figure in the world of radical environmentalism, first met Paul Watson on a high school graduation trip to Vancouver in 1984. Paul immediately put him to work on Sea Shepherd projects, among them three months of hard labor repairing the *Sea Shepherd II* after its release by the Canadian navy. Rod then served as a crew member on several Sea Shepherd campaigns, learning his trade from the master, but his first major exploit occurred in November 1986. He proposed to Paul a plan to sabotage the Icelandic whaling industry.

With Paul's support, Rod and companion David Howitt traveled to Iceland. On November 8, after weeks of reconnaissance, they drove to Iceland's main whale-processing station. Using only a large crescent wrench and a pair of heavy-duty bolt cutters, they thoroughly wrecked the whale-processing facility and, a few hours later, sank half of the four-ship Icelandic whaling fleet while the ships rested peacefully side by side in Reykjavik harbor. Their work finished, they made a clean escape.

Reporters by 1986 knew enough about antiwhaling protests to place a call to Paul Watson. Agreeably, Paul replied that the Sea Shepherd Conservation Society took public responsibility for the sinkings. (Paul, Rod said later, would take responsibility if a whaling ship were struck by lightning.) The subsequent publicity, including a Greenpeace boycott against Icelandic fish products, put enough pressure on Iceland to shut down its whaling industry. Not all went perfectly. Greenpeace carefully dissociated its name from the sinkings, and Iceland ignored Paul's repeated letters accepting responsibility, even when in January 1988 he flew to Iceland and demanded that the authorities arrest him.

Rod Coronado, meanwhile, gravitated toward radical groups such as Earth First! and the Animal Liberation Front, where he attracted enough arrest warrants and attention from the FBI that he now lives underground.

Rod had asked to come along on this campaign, Paul admits. Paul also says he strongly advised against it because the preparations were too public. The FBI, looking for Rod, no doubt tipped off the Customs Service, whose agents, flanked by the Harbor Patrol, pored over the two ships last night, checking the crew list and searching every closet and locker. The search party resembled an intergovernmental posse. It included customs, FBI and U.S. Treasury Department agents. All their opening and peering and lifting, however, proved in vain. Rod Coronado was not on board, and they eventually gave up the search.

The humor on the bridge this morning centers on the rough seas that had the agents (land animals like me, no doubt) terrified. As they left the *Edward Abbey,* first mate Peter Brown helped them make the tricky pitch-dark descent on the swaying rope ladder that dangled sometimes ten feet above their zodiac, rising and pitching with the waves. The last agent froze as he started down the ladder, clinging to Peter's jacket, unwilling to move, dangerously close to pulling Peter overboard, until with a powerful shove Peter launched him toward the zodiac below.

Without his helpful nudge, Peter swears, the agent would have dropped like a rock straight down into the bay.

⚓ ⚓ ⚓

Is anyone having fun yet? I'm still struggling, but Peter Brown is having a great time. Peter—not just first mate on the *Edward Abbey* but also cameraman and resident smart alec—holds the office of secretary-treasurer in the Sea Shepherd Conservation Society. He hangs out, on the rare occasions when he sits still, in the radio room, which resembles a small cramped box with only two ways out: the four stairs leading up to the bridge and, just a few feet away, a square hole in the floor, where a steep steel ladder leads down to the crew's quarters. A large map table and the hutch for our radiophone set take up one entire wall, while against the opposite wall Peter has built a combination bunk/workbench. The bunk hangs about three feet from the ceiling, like a student loft, creating space beneath for the workbench and its jumble of electronic gadgets. Cameras and photographic gear ride ingeniously in custom-built crevices that Peter has engineered everywhere. Crowded? Standing in the middle of the radio room, you bump into things wherever you turn. It may be cramped, but at least it comes equipped with a porthole, I note enviously.

Peter as first mate takes the unpopular midnight to 6:00 A.M. watch, with the result that his sleep consists mainly of catnaps, often squeezed in just before his shift. At any other time a steady flow of foot traffic tramps past his bunk. But as remarkable as his talent for insomnia is Peter's consistent cheerfulness. No one goes through the daily shipboard routine with more sheer pleasure than Peter Brown. Funny, wiry and fit, he likes to talk in overstatement, in an exaggerated high-pitched tone, as if every sentence contained a formal challenge. He almost forces you to respond, and then you're trapped in a war of wits, which he generally wins. I suspect

Peter Brown relaxes at his workbench in the radio room.

that his first act upon waking is to stretch, smile and say to himself loudly, "Looks like another great day, Peter."

Peter stops by to console me as I lie on my lower bunk, dizzy and nauseous, writing in my lab book, each stroke of the pen a small grim victory. With the aid of a metal hook, Meg and I have implemented an unspoken, permanent, open-door policy, which keeps our bunks visible at all times to anyone passing by. Indeed, the door opens directly onto the steel ladder leading up to the radio room, right beside the toilet, so we might as well sleep in a public convenience. Still, anything beats the six-by-eight-foot windowless crypt produced whenever the door bangs shut. An aged fluorescent lamp bolted to a useless narrow bedside desk gives off barely enough light to write by, when it works at all. I lie supine, lab book against my knees, knees jammed against the bottom of Meg's bunk.

Just moments after Peter leaves, an unusually large swell of nausea sweeps over me. Sick and weak, like someone spinning down into a bottomless whirlpool, I flick off the light, drop my pen into the gym bag and try not to throw up. Maybe thinking about Peter will help.

Peter leads one of the more fascinating lives among the *Edward Abbey* crew. Following a childhood spent mostly outdoors amid the seascapes of Cape Cod, he took his first job after college as a photographer, partly because it left lots of time to travel and ski. He seems to possess an inborn affinity for pleasure—one reason, perhaps, why people find him so likable—along with a pragmatic mind that lets him grasp the solution to almost any technical problem. He's happy to let you think his success is just good luck. A well-traveled photographer and an expert skier, Peter speaks fluent German, a trio of skills that just happened to be in high demand among American TV crews in Austria covering the 1976 Winter Olympics. Peter proved so indispensable that on his return from Europe he had three job offers waiting, and naturally he accepted the position that left him the most time free before it started. Like everyone else with free time in the 1970s, he drove out to California.

Smiles, wisecracks and an air of total competence seem so basic to Peter's character that on a desert island I suspect the palm trees would make him an offer. It seems preordained that, relaxing one day in a California bar, he fell to talking with a TV producer, who offered him a job for an upcoming network special: driving around the country with a television camera to interview ordinary people on the topic of imagination. Although Peter's previous work consisted almost wholly of still photographs, the filming he did for the special proved so skillful and inventive that his allotted five-minute segment expanded to twenty-five. He created the single spark of life in an otherwise moribund hour of television. Suddenly his phone wouldn't stop ringing.

His talents quickly led to jobs helping to start up two hit television series, *Real People* and *Entertainment Tonight.* This information solves the mystery of why Paul Watson is almost a regular guest on *Real People.* The answer, I know now, is Peter Brown. More important than any influence on guestlists, Peter helped invent and launch the influential genre known as "reality-based" television—leading to such current staples as talk shows, docudramas and home-video formats—where everyday events displace fiction, fast cuts displace extended narrative and real people displace paid actors. Television, however, always exacts its toll. Paul's latest appearance on *Real People* followed a segment featuring an elephant from the San Diego Zoo that paints pictures by holding the brush in its trunk. Since Paul would like to liberate every creature in every zoo in every country in the world, I hope he didn't watch.

Peter would probably be soaking in a hot tub somewhere right now if success in the world of television really mattered to him. He is part paradox and part maverick. Although he opposes any system that would restrict our powers to enjoy life, he also works hard and holds fast to a strict, if private, moral code. In this uncommon blend of hedonism and high seriousness, he closely resembles Paul, and indeed they are fast friends.

But friendships thrive on difference, too. Peter's TV work made him a lot of money. Putting down roots in L.A., he got married, bought a house with a beautiful view, had two kids and now cooks famous Sunday barbecues in his backyard to which celebrities bring their families. The cookouts, he says, are for his wife, a therapist, who doesn't share his impatience with Hollywood. Despite his success, Peter soon decided to leave network television. The iron law of the networks, he says, is "screw or get screwed." Free to make his own rules, Peter now runs an award-winning, independent film production company where he serves as one-man owner, producer, director, cameraman and writer.

Independence is the key for Peter. Each morning starts at a Santa Monica diner where he and Paul discuss Sea Shepherd business. It's a freedom inseparable from serious responsibilities. The birth of his two kids, Peter says, led him for the first time to start working to protect the environment. Now he devotes a good chunk of each year to filming Sea Shepherd campaigns. Beth Larsen turns out to be his only full-time employee, since he needs someone he can depend on—maybe someone even more practical than he is—to keep his business from unraveling while he makes his unpaid trips with Paul Watson into the far reaches of the globe. In addition to his commitment, talents and maverick independence, Peter must also have an abnormally low threshold for boredom and a very understanding wife, because this trip into the North Pacific is his fourth Sea Shepherd campaign in the last twelve months.

Later, forcing myself up on deck for fresh air, I hear Peter's normally wisecracking voice edged with anger. The L.A. firm he hired to repair and connect our radiophone—at a cost of some $1,300—has left us with a rat's nest of dangling wires. He studies the instruction booklet long into the afternoon, trying to hook us up but without success. The horizon has never looked so empty. If Peter can't get the radiophone to work, we can't contact shore. In a crisis—and crises seem a dead-cinch certainty given the state of our equipment and the nature of the ship-ramming business—we may be screwed for real.

⚓ ⚓ ⚓

We're a strange crew alone out here, pulled along behind the *Sea Shepherd II*. Paul and Peter are clearly in charge. Scamp, as chief engineer, handles almost every mechanical decision. Stuart runs the galley. Meg and Chris have the official title of deckhands. That leaves Jim and Ken to work the engine room. Ken, in his unchanging jeans, plaid shirt, open high-tops and ponytail, typifies the mix of dedication and quirky talent that runs through the entire crew. Twenty-eight, easygoing, he's a hydraulics specialist from L.A. called to help repair the *Sea Shepherd II* in Santa Cruz. He must have liked what he saw because he asked to join up. Then complications arose and it looked like he would have to back out, but at the last minute he tossed some clothes in a bag, called his boss, said good-bye to his girlfriend and his dog and took off. He doubted his job would be waiting when he returned.

The bosses at the steel mill didn't much care for him anyway, Ken says with a smile. He'd forced them to pay $1,200 a barrel to dispose of waste oil they used to dump for free. Or, he told them, maybe they'd like him to call Earth First!

Thinking about Ken, Stuart and Chris—in fact about all the unusual crew members aboard the *Sea Shepherd II* and *Edward Abbey*—I mention to Paul that the environmental movement needs people of differing talents and dispositions. It seems such a banal point that his disagreement astonishes me. The environmental movement, he says, is an illusion.

A momentary respite from nausea and dizziness at least lets me ask for an explanation.

There's no environmental movement, Paul says, because nothing is happening. People just give money to giant fund-raising organizations like Greenpeace in order to feel good, to buy a clean conscience on the cheap. He thinks it will take nothing short of a catastrophe—not just a Love Canal or a Chernobyl but an immense worldwide disaster—to change our relation to the planet. I get the feeling that he thinks the disaster is not too far away.

It's not surprising that people who make money by exploiting the environment have come to regard Paul as the enemy. His tactics are confrontational and sometimes violent. Yet, he denies that the destruction of inanimate objects is violence. Violence, he says, is an act of force directed against a living, sentient creature, and so ramming a ship doesn't count as violence.

Not everyone, of course, will buy this distinction. Paul also readily admits that his kind of nonviolence—acts of force directed against inanimate objects—upsets some people at least as much as traditional violence, perhaps more. Shootings, wife beating, child abuse, riots, drunk-driving fatalities and other violent acts have come to seem an inescapable cost of modern life. Politicians huff and puff against such violence, of course, but do we really expect to see much improvement? A kind of weary resignation takes over that closely resembles acceptance. An environmental activist who wrecks a bulldozer, on the other hand, perhaps a bulldozer used to destroy the few remaining traces of publicly owned wilderness, unleashes a frenzy of pious indignation against violence.

Paul's form of forceful nonviolence, he knows, has nothing to do with the civil disobedience associated with Thoreau, Gandhi and Martin Luther King Jr. He views Gandhian nonviolence as a brilliant tactic but an inadequate philosophy of life; the tactic worked in India because it provided the perfect weapon to use against the British and their smug moral superiority. In Stalin's Russia or Hitler's Germany, according to Paul, Gandhi wouldn't stand a chance. The totalitarians would just line him up against a wall and shoot him.

Gandhi, Thoreau and King, then, no matter how admirable their lives, strike Paul as inappropriate models in the struggle to protect the environment. The time left for effective action is just too short and the opposition too powerful. Each day for almost a decade, twelve square miles of Brazilian rain forest—the lungs of the planet—have been destroyed. This level of destruction really counts as progress: before 1985 the rain forest was disappearing three times as fast. At some point, because exponential forces are at work and entire ecosystems are disrupted, the damage becomes irreversible. How long before there's nothing left to save?

The enemy, too, is not always easy to find or attack. In the rain forest, blame lies not only with rich landowners and vast multinational conglomerates. Using roads cut by logging companies, landless peasants a few meals from starvation penetrate deep into the virgin forest, where they slash and burn to clear land for crops, pumping the air full of carbon dioxide and depleting the soil, so that soon they must push still farther into the forest and repeat the destruction. How do you feed such people if you chase them from the forest? A petition or sit-in directed against global disaster is not, in Paul's view, the right tactic. Moreover, he loves to point out that most people today *support* violence. Ninety percent of Americans backed the Gulf War against Iraq.

I can see, even in the mist-grey gloom, that Paul is warming to a familiar theme. At moments I get the feeling I'm on the receiving end of a speech he's given a hundred times before. Gazing past me, oblivious to my shaky hold on the handrail leading from the galley to the bridge, Paul launches into a story about a government ranger in Zimbabwe condemned by human rights groups for shooting a poacher. The poacher had just killed a protected black rhino. Paul recounts the episode like a skilled actor, at critical junctures almost taking over the voice and person of the beleaguered ranger.

"He said, 'Well, you know, if I was a policeman in Harari and I shot a bank robber who was running out of a bank with a bag of money, nobody would condemn that. Everybody would approve and applaud and put a medal on me and call me a hero because I am defending money.'"

Then, shifting into his own voice, Paul adds, with more than a trace of sarcasm, "In the defense of money, then, any kind of violence is justifiable in our society, but as to the defense of nature, no, it is not justifiable."

It doesn't bother Paul when politicians and newspapers label him a terrorist. He takes pride in knowing that the Sea Shepherd Conservation Society has saved thousands of whales, hundreds of thousands of dolphins and millions of seals, all without incurring a single criminal or civil conviction and without a single injury to his opponents or to the Sea Shepherd crews. The opposition is rarely so careful.

They have nearly killed him—several times. In 1977, on his second trip to protest the annual harp seal slaughter off Labrador, he handcuffed himself to a pile of fresh seal pelts awaiting retrieval. The retrieval process employs a winch that hauls each load of pelts over the ice by means of a long cable, hoisting them aboard when they reach the ship. Cheered on by the sealers, the winch operator aboard the Newfoundland sealing ship *Martin Karlsen* dragged Paul across the ice with the pelts, slammed him into the hull and dunked him repeatedly in the freezing Arctic water. At last a strap mercifully broke and he fell free, but only to drop into the icy sea where, literally paralyzed with cold, he was left to drown.

Environmentalists have been openly maimed and murdered. David McTaggart, the well-known Greenpeace leader, almost lost his right eye when French commandos in 1973 assaulted him aboard the small yacht that he sailed into the South Pacific in protest against the scheduled test of a French nuclear bomb.

"There hasn't been one person killed by an environmentalist," Paul states flatly. "It hasn't happened. Yet we're condemned as a militant, violent, terrorist organization. Those are just words."

The violence comes even from the governments who proclaim so piously against violence. In 1985 French government agents sank a Greenpeace ship in an explosion that also killed photographer Fernando Pereira.

"When the *Rainbow Warrior*, the Greenpeace ship, was sunk in New Zealand," Paul starts in again, "there wasn't a single leader of any Western nation who condemned that as an act of terrorism. And when it was brought up in the British House of Parliament, Maggie Thatcher said it was none of their concern. And when a Labour MP said, 'Well, it's a British ship with a British flag and a British captain and a British crew, sunk in a British Commonwealth port by members of the French government,' she said, 'I repeat, it is none of our concern.'"

"These people are hypocrites," Paul concludes with a smile of disdain. "The Bushes and the Thatchers and the Majors and the Mulroneys—they're all hypocrites, so what they say really is of no account to me."

⚓ ⚓ ⚓

Stuart, too, is feeling sick. Unfortunately he has no choice but to keep turning out meals below deck in the cluttered, overheated, odorous galley. Even up on deck, at the head of the steps leading to the galley, breakfast this morning smells so oppressive that I turn back, choosing to stay outside and breathe in diesel fumes. Invoking his managerial skills, Stuart has somehow imposed a system of order upon the jumble of provisions—the fruit is spoiling fast—but he also confesses to moments of panic.

The requirement to work in a small, stifling kitchen is bad enough. The rocking motion of the ship, however, feels ten times worse in the windowless galley with its pots, boxes, cans, knives, bottles and miscellaneous cookware forever sliding, swinging, tipping, rattling. The floor, slick with black diesel fuel, makes walking treacherous. So mostly you clutch at the floor-to-ceiling support pole or sit at a narrow Formica table, sharing bench space with an industrial-sized carton of carob clusters, trying not to watch the room move.

At times Stuart can't take it any longer, climbs outside for air and, despite the raw, wet weather, lies faceup on the deck. The grey skyline still encircling the ships is void of any object except the tossing sea. Sky and water share the same indifferent, slatelike hue.

"Reverse claustrophobia," Stuart mutters, gesturing at the horizon as he gets up off the deck, resigned and a bit desperate, and grips the round metal railing that guides him once more back down to his stove.

Meanwhile I retreat to my bunk to deal with the continuing seasickness, as if suffering a permanent world-class hangover. Popping a few more Dramamine tablets, I let my mind wander as my weight rocks on the bunk with the shifting of the ship. The motion makes me think of the pre-Socratic philosopher Thales, who argued that the single element composing the entire world was water. Another pre-Socratic, Heraclitus, wrote that "everything flows." I'm beginning to sense what they meant.

Everything on the *Edward Abbey* rolls and flows. Consequently, I need to learn how to roll and flow too. A small ship on rough seas offers a useful lesson. Even on land, if we employ the lenses of geological time, everything made out of matter—rock, river, mountain, glacier, continent—shifts its place and shape, rising and falling, waxing and waning, ebbing and flowing. Or so goes the philosophy of seasickness.

CHAPTER FOUR

UN-GREENPEACE

• • •

The most common mistake people make about Paul Watson, if they recognize his name at all, is to think that he works for Greenpeace. This is not correct: he helped to *found* Greenpeace, and Greenpeace later threw him out. More precisely, Paul was associated with Greenpeace from its beginnings in the early 1970s as a small antinuclear protest group in Vancouver, British Columbia. Vancouver served as an outpost for Americans opposed to the war in Vietnam, many of whom stood among the ten thousand people blocking the border between the United States and Canada in protest over the October 1969 American nuclear test blast on Amchitka Island. A Vancouver group calling itself the Don't Make A Wave Committee quickly organized a follow-up protest to oppose the next U.S. atomic test planned for Amchitka Island in 1971.

The Don't Make A Wave Committee responded to fears that had particular resonance in the Northwest. Amchitka Island lies at the upper tip of the Aleutian chain that swings north from Alaska, an area prone to earthquakes. A 1964 quake had killed more than 115 people in Alaska. Many people worried that the next test blast, hundreds of times more powerful than the explosion at Hiroshima, would set off earthquakes and tidal waves all along the West Coast. Even without a tidal wave, the blast would inflict significant damage because Amchitka Island was a national wildlife refuge, home to thousands of sea otters. It was also, however, American soil, and President Nixon, bred to the Cold War, did not intend to let a few thousand protesters or sea otters set back the defense of the free world. The atomic test would go on.

The organizing group for the Don't Make A Wave Committee, which included Robert Hunter, a young counterculture newspaper columnist for the *Vancouver Sun*, came up with a plan that was simple, lunatic and quite possibly suicidal: to block the explosion by sailing a charter boat, on the day of the test, directly into the waters around Amchitka Island. It took them over a year to find a captain in such need of money that he would risk sailing into a nuclear test zone. Finally the debt-ridden, foul-tempered, sixty-year-old captain of an idle halibut seiner, John Cormack, accepted the committee's offer. The Vancouver organizers quickly set about securing crew members for an old, dilapidated, peeling, wood-hulled clunker named after the captain's wife, the *Phyllis Cormack*.

Among the more persistent volunteers seeking a place on the twelve-person crew of the *Phyllis Cormack* was a muscular, twenty-one-year-old, knockabout seaman and sometime

Captain Paul Watson aboard the *Edward Abbey*

freelance journalist for the Vancouver underground press: Paul Watson.

The Don't Make A Wave Committee turned him down. Robert Hunter, in *Warriors of the Rainbow: A Chronicle of the Greenpeace Movement* (1979), offers some fascinating glimpses of the young Paul Watson. Watson, he writes, would have been a perfect candidate for the crew, except that he had North Vietnamese flags stitched to his jacket and wore "Red Power" and "Black Power" buttons and just about every kind of antiestablishment button going. The Don't Make A Wave Committee, thinking they had enough social misfits on their roster, wanted someone who looked respectable.

Undeterred, Paul got a position as oiler aboard the second ship headed for Amchitka Island, which left for the Aleutians after the *Phyllis Cormack* finally turned back because of bad weather and test delays. He was certainly needed. Although the young protest group had its share of freaks, hippies and acidheads, as well as some unorthodox lawyers, scientists, doctors and professors, they were very short on volunteers who knew anything about how to run a ship.

In autumn 1971 the Don't Make A Wave Committee officially changed its name to Greenpeace. Although they didn't succeed in stopping the second Amchitka atomic test, the widespread protests they helped to mobilize against American and French nuclear testing gave them overnight notoriety. Acclaim, however, did not translate into organizational stability. Until late in 1974 Greenpeace had no office, no telephone and no typewriter. In fact, with the death of founder Irving Stowe in October 1974, the Greenpeace Foundation for a time ceased to function. Its transformation into a well-focused environmental power occurred only in the mid-1970s. Before then, its sporadic growth more or less matched the pace with which the marriages of its members dissolved and careers unraveled in the rocky days following the Vietnam War.

Hunter's account makes it clear that the Greenpeace regulars did not hold Paul Watson in high regard. They found him impetuous and unpredictable, with a tendency to brag. Some were no doubt simply baffled by the martial arts buff, who could do such a flawless impersonation of John Wayne that they nicknamed him "The Duke." Paul must have felt some discomfort with his role as an outsider, for Hunter attributes to him during this period something of a persecution complex. Regardless, it was Paul Watson whom Hunter chose in 1975 to steer his zodiac as, in the most dangerous strategy Greenpeace had yet devised, they raced to put their bodies between a hunted whale and a Russian harpoon gunner poised to fire.

Paul split with Greenpeace in an emotional dispute three years later, in 1977. Accounts of the split differ. Paul clearly struck the new Greenpeace leadership as a liability in their quest for growth and power. It is fair to say that Greenpeace threw him out. It is also fair to say that between 1975 and 1977, the years that saw Greenpeace transformed from a Vancouver protest group into an international powerhouse, Paul Watson was crucial in creating the public perception of Greenpeace as scrappy, inventive daredevils ready to die in defense of the environment. Even the intrepid Robert Hunter credits Paul's courage and daring with calling forth a strength in Hunter he didn't think he possessed.

What images of Paul Watson linger from the Greenpeace years? There is Paul, young and slim, with a white cloth tied kamikaze-style around his forehead, its long white plumes snapping in the wind as he pilots his zodiac into the fray. There is Paul, his face fringed with a black beard, leaping from the zodiac onto the back of a freshly killed baby whale as a Russian harpoon boat roars toward them. There is Paul bundled against the Arctic cold as he organizes two Greenpeace campaigns to the Labrador Front to disrupt the annual seal pup slaughter. Many people, of course, deserve credit for the amazing work that Greenpeace has done, Bob Hunter chief among them, but no one did more to embody the Greenpeace myth than Paul Watson.

Today, however, he is one of Greenpeace's most vocal critics. Sour grapes? Perhaps. But consider that Greenpeace has now grown into a huge, multinational corporation with offices in twenty-four countries and some 5 million members worldwide. This giant lives mostly on donations—lots. It employs one thousand people and generates an annual income of over $150 million. These numbers prove heartening in that they emphasize the extent of worldwide concern about the environment. Indirectly they may lend support to Paul Watson's view that, in helping to found Greenpeace, he, like Dr. Frankenstein, created a monster.

He is not the only person to believe that Greenpeace has lost its way. Bjørn Økern, leader of the Greenpeace office in Norway from 1990 to 1992, asserts in his 1993 book, *Makt uten ansvar (Power Without Responsibility)*, that over two-thirds of Greenpeace employees work not on environmental campaigns but on fund-raising. For example, do people donating to the canvassers in Key West—whose arrival just happened to coincide with a well-publicized visit of the Greenpeace ship *Moby Dick*—really know that canvassers get to keep a hefty percentage of the money collected? The most prosperous national Greenpeace organizations pay the international council in Amsterdam a required royalty set at 24 percent of their net take from fund-raising.

Such practices help explain why a prestigious German weekly magazine, *Der Spiegel,* titled a 1991 exposé simply "Geldmaschine Greenpeace" ("Greenpeace Money Machine"). And the German press is not the only voice raised in criticism. In 1991 an American business weekly, *Forbes,* published a lengthy article on Greenpeace that questions its aims and methods. For example, *Forbes* criticizes the way that Greenpeace, in order to pass the 1982 moratorium on commercial whaling, packed the International Whaling Commission with half a dozen new members (including such nonwhaling powers as Antigua and St. Lucia), paid their $20,000 to $30,000 annual fees and handpicked their IWC representatives. Some charges in the article are groundless, and Greenpeace issued a point-by-point rebuttal. Most important in the *Forbes* critique, however, is the underlying view that Greenpeace, with its links to European left-wing politics, embodies a scarcely disguised disdain for capitalism and the free-market system. "Its philosophy," *Forbes* concludes disapprovingly, "is that pollution is a sin, not a cost, and should be outlawed, not taxed—even if that means shutting down industry."

The press war over Greenpeace makes strange bedfellows. The *Forbes* article opens, ironically, with a quotation from a person not generally known for his support of big business: Paul Watson. What the writers found useful is Paul's description of Greenpeace as a "myth-generating machine." Certainly Greenpeace soon set out a careful plan to manipulate the mass media and to boost its own image as a smokestack-climbing, harpoon-dodging, pollution-busting cadre of environmental fanatics. Companies like *Forbes*, of course, help to disseminate the very different and dominant imagery that extols the benefits of free-market capitalism. It might be useful to ask, then, what Paul sees as the current realities behind the machine-generated smoke and mirrors.

His view of Greenpeace reduces at some point to a kind of historical morality play in which the (good) rebel leaders who invent the revolution lose out over time to their bureaucratic (bad) successors. In effect the vision of the founders gets preempted and diluted by a second wave of organization wonks whose chief underlying mission, like the mission of bureaucrats everywhere, is to perpetuate their jobs. Protecting the environment dwindles from a passion to a college-approved career path with majors and electives and job fairs. This perhaps normal change is dangerous for the environment, in Paul's view, precisely because people who need to perpetuate their jobs have a vested interest in not alienating their source of funds. Environmental bureaucrats, he explains, above all tend to play it safe.

Paul believes that playing it safe—adopting a moderate style of compromise, cooperation and modest, incremental change—boils down to just another way of selling out the environment. Real protection of the environment, as opposed to feel-good gestures and fund-raising gimmicks, demands going out each day to do battle. Hard struggle, not moderation, is what will save the whales and the redwoods and the rain forest. Greenpeace, he believes, in its quest for funds and respectability, has lost the will to do battle.

Paul's line of attack bothers me, although I probably count as a moderate who might turn into a bureaucrat at any moment. I see room for many different environmental organizations with diverse styles and objectives, from The Nature Conservancy to the Environmental Protection Agency. Not everyone needs to do battle. Furthermore, Greenpeace has not retreated into quiescence. Michael Brown and John May, in *The Greenpeace Story* (1989), do a good job of indicating the worldwide impact of Greenpeace's direct actions, which continue to this day. Yet Paul's objections also seem forceful. Is it possible that Greenpeace could have also become a kind of huge environmental T-shirt factory—a money machine hijacked to make people feel good and to serve a safe, compromised, corporate agenda? Significantly, some mainline magazines such as *Forbes* and *Der Spiegel* now echo Paul's criticism.

Greenpeace at least offers a prime example of what the Sea Shepherd Conservation Society refuses to become. The organization that Paul set up after leaving Greenpeace is constructed so as to be immune to careerists, or "Greenpeace-proof." The Sea Shepherd Conservation Society thus employs no lawyers, no professional fund-raisers and no bureaucrats. Beyond its specific campaigns, Paul sees it as an informal training ground for volunteers, who will leave to found other organizations, like Alex Pacheco, founder of the animal-rights group People for the Ethical Treatment of Animals (PETA). The Sea Shepherd Conservation Society remains a place where activism is an appetite—a hunger and an obsession—rather than a job.

"There's no passion in this movement," Paul complains about the current state of environmental concern, which for the moment he's willing to call a movement. "We've been divorced from the natural world so long that the idea of protecting the environment is alien."

His criticism of Greenpeace, however well-founded, seems significant on a personal level, reflecting both the depth of his earlier attachment and the special bitterness of family conflict. Wars may simply put strangers on opposite sides: when the shooting stops, the hostilities begin to fade. Family conflicts, by contrast, make enemies of people who forever share a unique bond. The wounds never heal because they get rubbed raw, daily, by feelings of betrayal and revenge. A sacred trust has been broken, brother turns against brother, sister against sister, and the familial recriminations never end. Not surprisingly, Greenpeace has little use for Paul Watson.

⚓ ⚓ ⚓

It's been two days of grey sky, high seas and constant pounding. My slow movements as I shuffle around the ship make it clear how I feel, as if my pale green skin weren't enough. I still haven't been able to keep down food or water. The problem goes beyond my stomach, however. The *Edward Abbey* gets its fresh water from an onboard desalination system. I remember Scamp in Long Beach proudly showing me a large plastic cylinder and explaining how it produces drinking water by pumping the sea through a series of salt-removing filters. This morning he reports that the desalination system is broken. No fresh water. Scamp, Peter and Jim are putting in long, anxious hours struggling to bypass the trouble spot.

Feeling dangerously dehydrated, at about 6:00 P.M. I force myself to walk to the galley. When I get there, Paul and Peter are just sitting down to a stack of grilled cheese sandwiches. Stuart stands beside his stove with a hostile air, as if daring anyone to order more food. Paul, unconcerned, moistens his mottled yellow-black sandwich with a big dollop of catsup. Peter, who prefers mayonnaise, rips into his food with special gusto because, despite new frustrations with the freshwater system, today he finally got the radiophone to work. I pour a glass of lemonade, hunker in the corner where the narrow Formica table butts against the wall and try to focus on anything but cheese sandwiches.

There's no escape. Food is the subject of conversation. Strangely, the two ships linked by a long towrope are separated by irreconcilable philosophies of eating. While the *Edward Abbey* has stocked its galley with hamburger, chicken and (as I can't help noticing) cheese, the *Sea Shepherd II* is strictly vegetarian. Not just vegetarian. Almost the entire crew are vegans, people who reject all food and clothing that originate within the animal kingdom, from honey and butter to leather belts and shoes. Even ordinary bread is off-limits, because it rises thanks to a million expiring fungus cells. Paul, who likes hamburgers and grilled cheese sandwiches equally, interprets veganism as a form of philosophical lunacy.

There is more at issue than arguments about the merits of vegetables versus meat. Paul clearly chafes at living under implicit daily rebuke by the tattered collection of twenty-something idealists who now in effect run the *Sea Shepherd II*. Most vegans, he complains, are afflicted by a kind of political correctness and groupthink that extends even to their fondness for old clothes and dirt.

"It pisses me off," he says, reaching for his second grilled cheese sandwich. "All those clean T-shirts and shit I bought for them in Santa Cruz, and they still go around looking like the homeless."

As the conversation continues over pauses for mayonnaise and catsup, the *Sea Shepherd II* begins to sound like an extended sitcom, especially as Paul and Peter recall some of the characters from previous voyages. There was Lisa, in charge of the entire crew, so tough that everyone believed her when she claimed she killed her husband to get his fishing boat and stuffed his body in a crab trap. There was Fern, the nudist cook, who took long public showers on deck and once dallied with a male crew member directly below the bridge. She was furious when the event became shipboard gossip.

"Hey," Peter told her with his usual directness, "you fucked him right under the bridge and—what?—we're not supposed to *notice*?"

The episode of the Canadian Indians summons all of Paul's storytelling skills. The Indians approached him in 1992 with a plan to intercept the trio of Spanish ships—replicas of the *Nina*, *Pinta* and *Santa Maria*—retracing the voyage Columbus made five hundred years ago. They had organized a counterevent for the anniversary. Paul contributed a few finishing touches to their plan, volunteering the use of his ship, and eventually he and the Indians in the *Sea Shepherd II* confronted the *Santa Maria* in the waters off the island of San Sebastian. The Indians communicated to the Spanish captain their demand for a written apology. If the captain didn't apologize, they would sink his ship.

Stuart, at his post by the stove, can't quite believe what he is hearing. "You mean you planned to sink the *Nina*, the *Pinta* and the *Santa Maria*?"

"No," Paul replies patiently. "Just the *Santa Maria*."

At this point Peter can't resist jumping in. With his working knowledge of Spanish, he served as intermediary between the Indians and the captain of the *Santa Maria*. The captain, he explains, couldn't grasp why the Indians stopped him. He seemed to be under the impression that they wanted a tour of the ship.

"You don't understand," Peter says, his voice rising as he replays his role as go-between. "They don't want to tour your ship. They want to *sink* it. You know. Glub. Glub. Glub."

So the Indians got their written apology, later disembarking on San Sebastian to reclaim the island in the name of the native population. Comic guerrilla theater, if not exactly a coup d'état. For Paul, however, the real comedy of the voyage lay in the continuing daily contact aboard the *Sea Shepherd II* between the meat-eating, skin-clad Indians and the crew of vegans. He recalls the look of dismay on their faces when one of the Indians boasted to the vegans about setting out his traplines just before he left.

The dedicated young crew on the *Sea Shepherd II* sometimes genuinely annoys Paul. At other moments his stories convey the exasperation of a father who can't quite figure out why his kids dye their hair purple and wear their caps backward. He knows the conflict goes beyond style, and he knows he's locked in a standoff. With a resigned laugh he mops up the final pool of catsup with the crust of his last grilled cheese sandwich, lurches barefoot over the slippery, oil-coated floor and climbs up to the deck. As soon as Peter and Stuart leave, I rush to the sink and once more empty my stomach.

⚓ ⚓ ⚓

Overnight, somehow, my body has finally adjusted and I'm feeling a little better. The Dramamine must be kicking in. The sea, too, has turned calmer. It's a relief not to wake up woozy, dreading the light. Now, without nausea imminent, I find myself wondering why humans get seasick. Paul thinks the cause is psychological, linked with our fear of the sea. He says the Canadian navy used to give seasick sailors a bucket, a brush, and forced them to scrub the decks until they got over it.

The first maps were made not by overland travelers but by mariners, and I can see why. The sea, with its nonstop motion and absence of landmarks, threatens us with an utter loss of direction. We're off-balance, uncertain, disoriented. Still, seasickness doesn't seem wholly psychological. Maybe vertigo once served as a biological defense against kinds of movement that represented a danger to our survival, so that evolution finally hardwired it within us, like pain. It warned our tree-dwelling ancestors against acrobatics that might send them crashing to the ground as lunch for any passing saber-toothed tiger. After a few too many circles in the treetops, they suddenly just wanted to curl up in a fetal position and puke. Today seasickness is just an old alarm in our brains that goes off whenever the threat of losing our balance becomes serious. The trick for psychologists would be teaching us how *not* to get dizzy, like dancers or veteran sailors.

Meg is still badly seasick. I'm worried about her, especially because she's kept down even less fluid than I have. There's

Refueling the *Edward Abbey* was always a dangerous task and required plenty of help.

talk of shifting her to the *Sea Shepherd II,* which rides much steadier because of its size, weight and deep keel. The *Edward Abbey,* with its flat bottom, gets pitched around like a row-boat. The flat bottom also makes it easy to flip over. Its one big advantage over the *Sea Shepherd II* —speed—means we burn so much diesel that after about three days we need to refuel. The tanks must be nearly empty now. The *Sea Shepherd II,* by contrast, has more than forty days of fuel aboard. That's why it is towing us.

There's an urgency about refueling the *Edward Abbey* because a major storm would require us to cut the towline. The storm would batter us senseless if we had to cut loose and drift without fuel. Like the operation to attach the towrope, however, refueling requires us to ride up dangerously close behind the *Sea Shepherd II* and catch the line its crew tosses to us. Then they attach a fuel hose and pass it along the line from ship to ship. The job can be hair-raising. Scamp describes how once, in fifteen-foot seas, he stretched full-length from the bow of the *Edward Abbey* to retrieve a fuel hose as it dangled just out of reach.

"I thought it was all over," he says, not smiling.

Death lingers not too far from everyone's thoughts, I gather. With his terrifying earnestness, Jim greeted me on my first day aboard the *Edward Abbey* with a statement he attributed to Martin Luthur King Jr.: "A man who is afraid to die is afraid to live." It gives me no comfort. Fear, like dizziness, is an ancient biological defense. The question, then, is not whether you fear death but what you choose to do about it. Without fear, there's no courage—just boneheaded recklessness. But too *much* fear can be paralyzing. Thus, I'm in favor of scaling down my fears whenever possible. Like now.

Paul comes about as close as a person can to living without a fear of death. When I ask him about it, he replies that his sense of being connected to the earth—being an integral part of the continuum of life that has evolved over millions of years—has helped him get rid of fear.

"Once you see the world that way," he says, "it gets very peaceful."

⚓ ⚓ ⚓

It's not immediately clear how Paul came to see the world as he does. There are blank spots that he alone could fill in, and so far he hasn't filled them in publicly. He was born in Toronto in 1950 while his father was overseas fighting in Korea. The family, in the meantime, lived happily with Paul's maternal grandfather, Otto Larsen, a Danish exile and former prizefighter and lumberjack who taught art at the university. Like his grandfather, Paul unites contrary talents, and he especially loved to accompany him on regular visits to the Riverdale Zoo.

Paul says he remembers vividly the Blackwatch uniform his father wore on his return from the war in 1955. The return brought painful changes, especially to the five-year-old son who had never known his father. The family moved to a small, poor fishing village in New Brunswick, on Canada's east coast, a few miles from the U.S. border.

There were compensations. From ages five to fourteen, Paul lived with the sea as a daily companion. The family grew to a total of six children, with Paul the eldest. Despite their poverty, he lived what he calls an "idyllic" childhood, including regular fishing expeditions and contact with the local Canadian marine biology station. One summer he spent swimming in a nearby pond that he shared with a not-too-territorial beaver. The idyll ended in 1963 when his mother died after a miscarriage. Paul was thirteen, and the loss proved devastating. Within a year his father moved the family inland to London, Ontario, on the corridor from Toronto to Detroit.

Without his mother's gentle intercession, Paul and his father found themselves in constant conflict. A grieving teenage son in the 1960s would not find it easy to communicate with a father whom he still regarded as something of an interloper. First Paul had left his beloved grandfather, and now he had lost his mother. And his father? Returned just eight years from the battlefield, he was left alone to raise six children. Conflict eventually reached the breaking point. Paul says he didn't so much run away from home as drift away. At sixteen he signed up to work as a tour guide at Expo 67 in Montreal, and then rode the rails west—clear across Canada—to Vancouver, British Columbia.

Vancouver provided a reunion with the sea, and for the next six years Paul spent hitches with various ships and navies, advancing from deckhand to oiler to able seaman. He saw brief service with the Canadian Coast Guard. Meanwhile, as he soaked up maritime training, he also managed to fit in a semester of linguistics and communications at Simon Fraser University, with some freelance writing for Vancouver's counterculture weekly, *Georgia Strait.* Most important, during the same year that he served as an eighteen-year-old deckhand on the Pacific and Indian oceans, he also joined a group of Vancouver activists who were planning to protest the U.S. nuclear test blast on Amchitka Island.

Several years later in 1971, when this informal group reorganized to fight the Amchitka Island nuclear test under its fateful new name Greenpeace, twenty-one-year-old Paul Watson, his jacket plastered with protest buttons, was among its most active volunteers.

The ensuing six years with Greenpeace, 1971 to 1977, belong to the modern history of the environmental movement. The band of activists, making it up as they went along, soon shifted their focus from antinuclear protest to the environment, living on the edge of poverty, often down-and-out, but revitalized by a sense of their power to change the world. Organized episodes range from high comic symbolism—as when Greenpeacers on a Vancouver bridge pelted a passing French destroyer escort with marshmallows and mushrooms—to frightening confrontations. Thus in 1975, at the height of the Cold War, Paul played a major role when Greenpeace for a second time chartered the rundown *Phyllis Cormack* to track and confront the immense Russian whaling ship *Dalniy Vostok*.

Whales, indeed, were becoming central to Paul's thinking. One key moment occurred in 1973 when, along with Greenpeace pal David ("Walrus") Garrick, Paul drove a tattered pickup truck from Vancouver to South Dakota to join the American Indian Movement at Wounded Knee. Paul made his way to the surrounded Indian compound by crawling on his stomach through the snow past lines of FBI agents, U.S. marshals and heavily armed National Guard troops. Once inside, he served as a medic. When the sixty-nine-day siege ended, with two Indians killed and one federal marshal seriously wounded, the Oglala Sioux initiated him as a warrior brother and gave him the Sioux name Grey Wolf Clear Water. Here at Wounded Knee, in a vision during a sweat lodge ceremony, he also saw his destiny: to protect the great whales that, like the buffalo before them, were being hunted down and eradicated.

This crucial vision makes Wounded Knee a deeply personal as well as historical event. But is it more? Did it generate not only a vision of his future but also something like a new identity? Wounded Knee, I suspect, was not so much a conversion experience—Saul reborn on the road to Damascus—as a confirmation, a gathering-together of the spirit, an experience that turns an entire life toward one goal with renewed purpose and unshakable conviction. Paul is not like the introspective souls who spend their lives in therapy or meditation searching for their own hidden, personal identities. He expresses who he is in action, unfolding along with events, so full of contrary impulses and powers as to seem, like Grandfather Larsen, a contradiction. What remains consistent are his passions, values and beliefs. He strikes me as an irreverent, cosmic, biological democrat.

"Christ, Mohammed and Buddha," he claims, "were primates, cousins to the chimpanzee and the mountain gorilla, just as we are all children of a species of naked simians."

Cousins of the chimpanzee and mountain gorilla, of course, are not immune from repressed desire or buried conflict. Does Paul's dislike of authority replay his feeling for an overbearing father? Tony Watson, his father, actually came along once as cook on a Sea Shepherd campaign at Paul's invitation. The crucial conflicts in Paul's life are not concealed—though, like everyone, he may carry some forgotten scars—but utterly public. Suburbanites and city dwellers like me might get the deepest insight into Paul Watson simply from a summer spent swimming every day in an undisturbed beaver pond.

By the summer following the daily swims with his wild companion, Paul reports, the beaver was gone, perhaps shot, trapped or poisoned by developers. Paul was eight when he sent off for membership in a children's organization called the "Kindness Club," which promoted the humane treatment of animals. He recruited his brothers and sisters to roam the woods with him, as benevolent outlaws, setting free creatures caught by trappers. Years of psychoanalysis aren't necessary to explain why someone should feel a profound love of the earth and a passion to oppose the human mistreatment of nature. We would do better to begin seeking out the historical and psychological causes of our indifference.

⚓ ⚓ ⚓

The radiophone operators at station KMI sign off with a phrase I've grown to like. Most of the calls, of course, come from ships at sea. Some calls originate on luxury liners, but I'd guess that isolated fishermen days or weeks from land place most of them. Anyway, at the end of a call the KMI operator breaks in, asking if the caller has any other numbers to dial and finally signs off with the standard line, "Have a safe watch."

At sea someone is always on watch—a lonely job late at night or in the cold hours before dawn. Paul seems to relish the solitude on his normal 8:00 P.M. to midnight watch. He's sitting alone at the bridge as the half moon lays down a path on the wrinkled black surface of the ocean. A few icy stars shimmer overhead, while dark clouds mass like distant mountains against the even darker horizon. In the warm yellow glow of the bridge Paul looks like a contented hermit, his stockinged feet propped on either side of the wheel, listening to Irish folk songs on the stereo and reading the Yukon poems of Robert Service.

"It is the nature of a warrior to act," Paul claims. Maybe we should think about keeping watch as a form of action. Milton ends his famous sonnet on blindness with the line "They also serve who only stand and wait." If waiting counts as service, keeping watch must count too. Milton wrote the sonnet in his forties, his blindness nearly total, wondering how a blind poet could accomplish anything of value. He decided that we can serve simply by standing still—alert, waiting, upright, watching. Who knows when the crucial moment may come? Keeping watch doesn't sound very heroic, but vigilance is the opposite of falling down or falling asleep or deserting your post. The idea would be that we protect the environment by constantly keeping watch.

Then, again, waiting and watching can constitute a cowardly or even criminal failure to act. A bystander who watches a crime perpetrated and who fails to intervene is, by law, a criminal. Paul grew disillusioned with Greenpeace mainly because he felt it had lost the will to act. The breaking point came in 1977, on his return from the second harp seal campaign he had organized for Greenpeace, when the sealers nearly killed him with repeated dunkings in the icy waters off Newfoundland. Earlier in the protest, Paul had confronted a seal hunter on the ice who was raising his bloody club to smash the skull of another baby seal. Paul told him to stop. The hunter ignored him. As the club swept downward, Paul grabbed the hunter's arm, twisted the club free and tossed it into the freezing North Atlantic.

Greenpeace had always professed to follow the Quaker-based nonviolent philosophy of bearing witness. Bearing witness means opposing by exposing, not by bearing arms. The notorious Quaker opposition to violence, for example, has removed Quakers from key conflicts such as the American Revolution, as Benjamin Franklin discovered when he sought unsuccessfully to enlist their direct aid against the British. On his return from Newfoundland, barely recovered from near-death at the hands of the sealers, Paul was called before the Greenpeace board by Dr. Patrick Moore, a biologist newly installed as president.

Patrick Moore and Paul Watson already had a long history of run-ins, although Paul had recently backed him when Moore first challenged Robert Hunter for the presidency of Greenpeace. Political struggles had begun to fracture the leadership of the increasingly famous organization, whose membership had recently shot up from a handful to some eighty thousand. Like the other directors, including Hunter, Moore felt that Paul's impulsive, independent, warrior style hurt the prospects of an expanding organization. As he stood before the board, Paul was charged with theft of the Newfoundland sealer's club. He couldn't believe it.

"You don't seem to understand what Greenpeace is all about," said a lawyer new to the board.

"No," Paul replied, as he walked out, "I guess I don't."

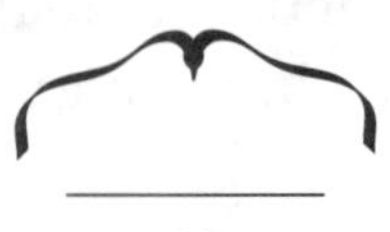

CHAPTER FIVE

TELEVISION AND ANESTHESIA

• • •

Yesterday our sewage system backed up, Scamp ran a high fever and Meg spent twenty-four hours in her bunk ashen with seasickness. Today, among the unimpaired, I spend much of my time on the bridge, on watch, in the big white captain's chair that sways unsteadily on a metal pole directly behind the wheel. Like a ponderous metal brontosaur climbing a low hill, the *Sea Shepherd II* labors up each huge rolling swell and then crashes awkwardly down the other side. While the *Sea*

Chris Maenz, Scamp and Meg Larsen (left to right) enjoy a quiet moment on the aft deck of the *Edward Abbey*.

Shepherd II rocks slowly forward and back, the *Edward Abbey,* pulled along passively behind, rocks at a faster pace, not just back and forth but side to side, too. Even with the choppy sea transformed into vast torpid swells, life onboard the *Edward Abbey* resembles days spent in the maw of a perpetual motion machine.

Although the weather today is much better, the desalination system is not. Scamp, Chris, Jim, Ken and Peter have been poring over the instruction book. They have torn the system apart and put it back together a dozen times. Finally, they used the newly functional radiophone to call the manufacturer in L.A., who suggested a few obvious adjustments and said to call back after the weekend. Four days from land, no fresh water and he says call back after the weekend! At the moment, however, we defer worrying. Maybe Paul figures we can borrow fresh water from the *Sea Shepherd II,* assuming, of course, that *its* purification system doesn't break down.

Later we approach the edge of a downpour visible from several miles away. After days with no water for showers, carrying deep in our pores the sweat and grime and stench of round-the-clock labor, we all dash to the forward deck, grabbing soap and towels, ready to strip naked for an all-gender frolic in the rain and suds. But only a teasing sprinkle falls, so with regret we put off cleanliness for yet another day. Scamp, the worst case, gives up and scrubs the grease off his arms and neck with a bucket of saltwater.

⚓ ⚓ ⚓

One crucial feature of Paul's work, I'm learning, is the use of film, which explains why Peter Brown plays such an important role. It's not just that they're close friends. Paul's reliance on television and film reflects his understanding of theorist Marshall McLuhan, whose work he studied at Simon Fraser University. McLuhan's ideas, in fact, contributed much to the early strategy of Greenpeace. Bob Hunter believed that the new planetwide mass-communication system—McLuhan's electronic global village—marked a decisive turn in human history: the moment when a single person or single group might suddenly command the entire world's attention. A fresh concept or image could instantly circle the earth. Most important for the environment, rapid electronic communication would permit access to what Hunter called "the collective mind of the species that now controls the planet's fate."

McLuhanism, soon merged with cybernetics, remains heady stuff, and Greenpeace explored its implications like a rock-and-roll Columbus of the airwaves. They even adopted their zippy new name for its aid in electronic public relations—*Greenpeace* suggesting a hip marriage of antinuclear sentiment and ecology. Hunter wanted what he called "mind bombs": powerful images delivered via the mass media to restructure consciousness. As a print journalist bred on the Gutenberg revolution, he was perhaps especially sensitive to McLuhan's emphasis on the new power of visual imagery. Although he remained loyal to his typewriter until finally resigning from the *Vancouver Sun* in 1975 to become full-time president of the Greenpeace Foundation, Bob Hunter as activist early on enlisted the power of electronic images. The Vietnam War is often called the first war fought on television, and Greenpeace set out to bring the struggle for the environment directly into the world's living rooms.

Paul not only shared in this strategic thinking about electronic media but also revealed an unusual gift for dreaming up images to woo the camera. When in 1975, along with David Garrick, he masterminded the first Greenpeace expedition to the Labrador Front, one essential aspect of the strategy was pictorial: activists in bright orange arctic survival suits clambering over ice floes to spray the fuzzy white harp seal pups with green dye. The dye would not only make the pelts commercially useless but also stand as a visual signature for Greenpeace. The campaign, Paul calculated, would generate images that almost cried out for color television.

As it happened, the expedition ran into terrible storms and insoluble logistics problems, not to mention carloads of incensed Newfoundlanders. The spray pumps found use only as a bargaining chip, when Bob Hunter renounced them in a fruitless effort to win the goodwill of local sealers. (A cagey pragmatist, he learned that the Canadian government had just passed an order making it illegal to paint seals.) When Paul, in 1979, finally got a chance to use spray pumps on his third expedition to the Labrador Front, he had already left Greenpeace and altered the dye to an equally photogenic red. Red dye or green makes no difference: the strategy looked beyond saving a few individual seal pups. If you can figure out how to attract the camera with colorful, fascinating, alarming images, you might galvanize public opinion and eventually save an entire species.

Photographs, then, became a crucial weapon in the fight to protect the environment, a weapon that sometimes shaped tactics. On his second campaign to Labrador in 1977, for example, Paul as expedition leader agreed to a visit at their base camp by French film star and animal-rights activist Brigitte Bardot. Bardot, in fact, brought along a retinue of at least forty-five European journalists. Although reluctant to be upstaged, even perhaps unaware of Bardot's iron determination to protect the animals she loved, Paul quickly recognized the value of her symbiotic relation to the camera. Soon a photo of the former sex kitten snuggling cheek to cheek with a white harp seal pup appeared on the cover of France's equivalent of *Time* magazine. This single photo, Paul claims, directly influenced the European Common Market in its decision to ban Canadian seal pelts.

Every well-prepared Sea Shepherd press conference now includes its quota of movie stars. When a reporter complained about a touch of cynicism in the use of celebrity spokespersons, Paul pointed out that reporters otherwise would not attend his press conferences.

"We don't set the rules," he told one newspaperman. "We just play the game."

The picture of Paul Watson in docile agreement to play by the rules doesn't quite carry conviction. Indeed, he crafts all his public campaigns for maximum electronic impact. A three-man crew from Yorkshire Television currently fills almost an entire room of the *Sea Shepherd II* with its cameras, lights and sound gear. I sense, however, that Paul's thinking has changed since McLuhan's concept of an electronic global village first promised a revolution in consciousness. He knows firsthand how conservative the mass media are, despite their reputation for liberal leanings. The issue is not whether a specific broadcaster harbors left-wing sympathies. No matter what their personal politics, no matter how many liberals hold network jobs, individuals alone cannot overcome a conservatism inherent in the mass-communication system.

What conservatism? Where enormous sums of money are at stake, an equally vast and impersonal pressure develops—something like the force of gravity—conspiring to keep things in their present alignment. A presidential election, a shift in congressional leadership or a new regulatory commission makes no more real difference than the almost irrelevant consumer choice between a Ford and a Chevrolet. The choice between buying a car and riding the bus, on the other hand, is a genuine alternative with serious consequences for the environment—an alternative that will never get equal time on television. The mass media always sustain the deep structure of the status quo.

The job of a second-generation McLuhanite activist has thus become especially complex for two more reasons. First, all media are now electronic media, even newspapers, which depend on photos, graphs, satellite feeds, word processors and immediate, worldwide communications. Bright colors splashed across the masthead and three-dimensional pie graphs on the front page make McLuhan's famous distinction between hot and cool media lose much of its point. Second, environmental protest is old news. Paul must somehow induce the inherently conservative mass media—simply by following their visual logic, hunger for novelty and capitalist principles—to disseminate a heretical and revolutionary message: information that undermines the status quo and threatens the security of the mass media themselves.

I have no idea how Paul plans to induce an act of unconscious self-betrayal by the mass media. It can't be done just by ramming a driftnet ship. I suspect he knows that the force of gravity won't betray itself. You must simply use its physics for your own purposes, as in judo, which for Paul perhaps means a decision to live out, with the intensity and integrity of high drama, a way of life that people eventually cannot ignore. A single human life, on rare occasions, can tap the power of exponential change, altering the course of history. It's certain that Paul won't stop attacking whalers and driftnetters. The longer he sticks to his dangerous work, the better the chance that one day ordinary people around the world will pick up on what he is all about. On that day, the world will change.

⚓ ⚓ ⚓

Meg has begun to rally, although her sweatpants hang so loose she must have lost ten or fifteen pounds. In fact the emerging good weather gives everybody a lift, and I sense almost a spirit of mischief in the air. I'm sure of it when we spot a sailboat far off the port side. While Jon Huntemer on the *Sea Shepherd II* makes radio contact with the sailboat, the *Edward Abbey* crew crowds onto the bridge to eavesdrop over the open channel. We learn that they are several weeks out of Hawaii and delivering the sailboat to San Francisco. The sight of our two black ships—one with military silhouette—at first took them aback, but they, too, seem starved for conversation. Jon trades nautical information with the sailboat captain as the *Edward Abbey* crew continues to listen in.

Patience and thoroughness, Jon's great virtues as a captain, unfortunately do not always make for spirited conversation. He talks in a painstaking monotone that seems to drag on forever, and in the sailboat captain he has apparently met his linguistic twin. Eavesdropping from the *Edward Abbey* is like being trapped at the Olympics of Boredom. We would have tuned out, except there's a berserk comedy in overhearing a conversation so slow and banal that each sentence threatens to die in midair.

It is permissible to listen over the open channel, of course. That's how the custom agents knew to board us just moments before we were scheduled to leave Santa Cruz. Eavesdropping over the ship-to-shore radiophone, however, is punishable by a $10,000 fine. After days at sea, such legalism frightens no one. Besides, you *have* to eavesdrop in order to break in and contact the KMI station operator. Jon's endless exchange has simply whetted our desire for fresh human voices, and so, later, as Peter waits to contact the KMI operator, we can't help but notice when a man's voice cuts through the static: "Fuck you, bitch."

Instantly, at least in the eyes of the FCC, the captain and five bored crew members in the radio room are transformed into criminals. But *not* listening is more than human nature could bear. As Peter struggles to improve the sound, we hear someone named John engaged in berating his wife or girlfriend, Joan. It seems Joan, irritated by John's long absences from home, has grabbed the kids and the credit cards and left on a Pacific cruise. The radiophone lets you hear only half of a conversation—John's half—but the one-sidedness creates an impromptu game requiring us to imagine Joan's response. We have a lot of filling in to do.

There are some great lines. (John: "I didn't leave the kids, I left *you*.") John, we learn, has been spending too much time with Mary—whom he now dismisses as a "slut"—which is the reason why Joan has decamped on a cruise with the kids and the credit cards. Here is real life. With each new revelation, Meg openly begs Joan to dump him, inspiring Peter, in a spirit of cross-gender competition, to start up an extemporaneous defense of John.

"Dammit, she's going to cry," Meg worries. "I know she's going to cry."

"Cry, you bitch! Cry!" Peter does his best rendition of a pig.

Eventually the contest is over. We can't hear Joan, of course, but John's simpering attempt to soothe her leaves no doubt about the tears. Meg reacts as if she has just overheard Eve caving in to the snake: another defeat for women. The drama, however, holds a final ambiguous moment worthy of the finest soap opera, leaving everyone eager to intercept another call tomorrow. John's last words go exactly like this: "I love you, Joan. I love you, Joan. Joan. Joan? Joan?"

⚓ ⚓ ⚓

A radio call from the *Sea Shepherd II* tells us they've just spotted a pod of dolphins off the starboard side. At first I can't locate them, but suddenly nine or ten dolphins race past the ship in a chorus of fluid curves. For a week we've had no sign of life except for one intermittent, faithful albatross, who swoops and skims along the huge swells, following the contour of the water. An albatross is a large bird that spends its adult life at sea, drinking seawater and feeding on squid, returning to land only to breed. On windy days it can glide for hours without moving a wing. When the waves subside and the air is too calm for gliding, the albatross then settles down on the placid surface of the sea for a nap.

Appearing out of nowhere and moving through the water with unearthly grace, the dolphins seem like a delegation of minor deities. No wonder Dionysus—the god of fertility, wine and ecstasy—often appears in Greek art with his arm around a dolphin. Now I understand better what Peter means when he reassures his young daughter about his frequent and dangerous absences at sea by telling her that God is a dolphin. Her Sunday school teacher, doubtless sensing a lost cause, says at least it's an advance over her father's previous statements.

Peter, whatever his grasp on theology, is a wizard at fixing things. His expertise seems to extend to anything that comes with an instruction book, like the radiophone. It's a relief to know that we can get calls through in an emergency. Moreover, Peter's mere presence here is reassuring. He seems fully enmeshed in the network of life on land, which is all I really know. Once, while he was collaborating with Scamp on a particularly risky bit of shipboard work, I heard him yell in his high-pitched seriocomic style, "Hey! Be careful! I've got two kids waiting for me at home."

Peter's notion that God is a dolphin would make a good story. Why is it that stories hold such universal appeal? Despite all the pressures to make us think in logic and propositions, humans seem born for narrative. Every culture has its myths, bedtime stories and nursery rhymes. *Hickory dickory dock. The mouse ran up the clock. The clock struck one and down he run*. The rhyme helps, even the cracked grammar, but it would mean nothing without the mininarrative of the mouse and its 1:00 dash. The story makes all the difference.

Stories hold a prominent place not because we crave entertainment or have grown addicted to TV. A fascination with narrative seems part of the new biological equipment our ancestors developed about one hundred thousand years ago, when they added layers of neocortex, relocated the larynx and invented speech. We use stories, from comic books to epic poems, in order to make sense of the world. Injure the right hemisphere of the brain and a person can still talk, but can't make sense of narratives—or big chunks of the world. When experimenters block contact between the right and left hemispheres of the brain, the talkative left hemisphere starts making up stories to explain an apparently incomprehensible decision taken by the mostly mute right hemisphere. Specialists call it confabulation, but we are all confabulators. A race with no stories would quickly die out.

This is where Peter comes in. His job, he says, is just to get it in focus. Beneath the wisecrack, he knows the importance of pictures in the Sea Shepherd campaigns. Yet herein lies a paradox. Maybe electronic mind bombs have begun to lose their power.

Maybe pictures have become too common. An environmental strategy that centers on strong images circulated by the mass media perhaps miscalculates the process by which people actually come to make deep-down, lasting changes. Deep change is hard. It isn't reinforced by the pleasure that accompanies much new learning. In fact it often requires painful *un*-learning. Can a mind bomb give pleasure or sustain the difficult daily changes that environmental restoration will demand?

Furthermore, Americans have grown insatiable in their need for televised spectacle—but also numb. Television feeds on fresh images, like the latest plane crash or sex scandal, but we soon forget yesterday's stale image and hunger for a new pageant. Television is an ideal consumer product because its content must be endlessly replaced and hence endlessly replaceable, like breakfast cereal. Yet a medium that subsists on endless and interchangeable replacements may finally neutralize its power to alter human consciousness. The danger is quite real that a Sea Shepherd campaign will generate simply one more fading news clip or one more transient, stale photo. What, then, about Peter's role?

The theory I'm nursing along, privately and no more than half-seriously, is that Paul Watson should be considered one of this century's great unknown performance artists. He would no doubt reject this view at once, because it seems to trivialize his defense of the environment, but performance art and environmental defense are hardly trivial. Moreover, the early Greenpeace years certainly provided Paul a training ground in guerrilla theater. My theory, then, would hold that he uses ships and oceans and ice fields as a stage on which to create a gigantic improvisational artwork. He's telling a kind of extended, if unusual, story.

Perhaps we should think of him as a colleague of the Italian artist Christo, who wraps whole buildings with fabric and has created a cloth fence that runs for miles along the coast of California. Art not for the museum, but for the earth. Art that reaches out and enfolds us in its mysterious unfinished narrative, that seeks to change us by its power to think the unthinkable.

Paul knows that his ongoing story inevitably includes the fascination of blood and death. That's another reason why the reporters cover him. Yet what is his alternative? He opposes people so incensed by his values and tactics that they regularly threaten his life. Performance art and storytelling often use whatever raw materials lie at hand. Maybe an activist—an Earth Warrior—who risks his life in death-defying struggles on behalf of the environment is creating a compelling new and improvised nonfiction narrative.

The unfolding story—not the separate, fading visual images—would be what holds the power to give us pleasure and sustain us through the deep changes ahead. Such a life's work might just hold the power of myth.

This train of thought moves through the back of my mind as I stand with Peter beside the zodiac strapped down on the aft deck. While we talk, Peter works steadily, repairing the braided rope that weaves through grommets around the perimeter of the small craft. It is tedious, exacting, thankless work. The zodiac serves as our only lifeboat—a cramped lifeboat at best, and I suspect it won't hold everybody. It may also see duty against the driftnet ships. The braided rope might mean the difference between someone's hanging on and falling off. As could be expected, the rope is frayed, the grommets split or ripped.

Peter's skills are amazing. I am mesmerized by the patience with which he forces open the braided strands and feeds in each segment of new rope, tying off the splices with tight loops of nylon thread. His only tools are a pair of needle-nose pliers and a wedge-shaped knife that Paul received from the Dalai Lama, supposedly a big supporter of the Sea Shepherd Conservation Society.

Still working at the braids, Peter talks about how the birth of his two kids woke him up to an awareness that they would live in a world almost stripped of wildlife.

"I want to be able to tell them when they're twenty," he says in a rare moment of total seriousness, keeping his eyes on the rope, "that I was out here doing something, trying to stop it."

⚓ ⚓ ⚓

Normally Peter sticks to the role of jester, often joined by Stuart, who has taken to calling himself, with a Jamaican lilt, "Galley-mon." Galley-mon's dinners are a hodgepodge of politics, philosophy and slapstick. Tonight Paul begins a long discourse on how water acts uniquely like a living creature. Meg, who cannot be intimidated and who also teaches high school science, breaks in to correct Paul's assertion that water is heavier as a liquid than as a solid. With a detailed molecular analysis, she explains that ice is not lighter than water but *denser.*

"I knew that," Peter grunts, going into his pig act, head down, lips close to his bowl.

"Yeah," grunts Paul. "I knew that."

Meg, unimpressed, adds an even more stunning description of why water at the bottom of a lake never drops below four degrees centigrade.

"I knew all about that," Peter grunts again.

"Yeah, me too," grunts Paul.

Meanwhile Galley-mon, working with only a lasagna pan and an oven that rocks with the motion of the ship, has somehow produced a birthday cake for Jim, which of course generates predictable jokes about why Jim gets special treatment. It's an odd cake, high in the middle, low at the sides, but impressive when you consider that every object in the rattletrap galley rocks and tips and slides. Cake batter has a zero chance of coming out level. Stuart's eyes widen in disbelief as Paul cuts himself an enormous square of cake directly from the center. Scooping it out with his hand, Paul says he doesn't like the "hard shit" around the edges.

Stuart's recourse is to run for his camera. He returns to snap an incriminating shot. Unashamed, Paul poses in front of the rectangular cake with its gaping center and mugs a wide grin as Peter points an accusing finger at the captain.

So it goes, with Peter usually playing for laughs, keeping everyone both loose and connected, nothing too serious, just a shipload of slightly loony activists out to bump a driftnetter and shoot some film. The act is only part hoax. Beneath the jokes, Peter remains deeply cynical about the television networks with their appetite for violent pictures, whether it's endless replays of Rodney King getting beaten up by L.A. cops or two ships colliding at sea.

Paul ends the meal with a riff about violence in which he slides from condemning widespread American support for the so-called antiseptic Gulf War ("How many Iraqis killed? A hundred thousand? Two hundred thousand?") to attacking George Bush's "cowardly and despicable" desertion of the Kurds whom he left for the defeated Iraqis to slaughter.

"Violence," Paul continues, "is the only way that oppressed people ever throw off the chains of the oppressors, but the oppressors, of course, want to look like they've got this high moral position where they say, 'No, no, you can't condone violence,' when all the time, of course, it's violence that they use to keep the oppressed with their faces in the mud. Look at the American Indians, with an unbroken record of nonviolence from 1890 to 1973, when all that time the government oppressed them so terribly they were almost exterminated. And it was only after they resisted at Wounded Knee in 1973 that the North American Indians gained any sense of dignity and self-respect. ..."

⚓ ⚓ ⚓

Paul has good reason for distrusting journalists. He is not just misquoted—the fate of every public figure—but deliberately misrepresented. During his campaign to stop the annual harp seal hunt, a reporter asked him how he felt about rumors that he would be shot. Paul replied that things were pretty bad if people had to shoot those with whom they disagreed and that such people were no better than barbarians. The local Newfoundland newspaper ran this catchy headline: WATSON CALLS NEWFOUNDLANDERS BARBARIANS.

⚓ ⚓ ⚓

At breakfast we discuss whether Joan and John should consider therapy. It's not entirely an innocent question, because Peter's therapist wife gave him as leisure reading on the campaign D. W. Winnicott's *Home Is Where You Start From.* She thinks Paul, too, would benefit from therapy, but Paul tells her that he's happy, so why should he see a therapist? Of course, maybe he's not *really* happy, or maybe his happiness is a delusion, or perhaps he could be a lot happier. None of this works with Paul.

"I've had a good life," he tells Stuart, adding in a typical leap, "I don't believe in old age."

The floor of the galley is still slick with a dark film of diesel fuel. With walking treacherous, especially given the constant lurch and roll of the ship, I've learned to move with a controlled slide as I collect my daily soy milk and granola, like a car fishtailing around a corner. Not believing in old age is fine for Paul, I'm thinking, but why drag me into it? How about settling for a vigorous fifty? At least until I'm off the ship.

Meanwhile, after finishing my granola—the only food I dare to eat, and nobody else wants the soy milk—I try a few carob clusters from the supply donated by a Santa Cruz health food store. I've been thinking about Joan and John. Paul, now divorced, seems an archetypal wanderer, someone for whom settling down means dying by slow degrees. He tells how Edward Abbey—renegade Forest Service ranger, novelist and anarchic environmentalist—woke up in the cancer ward, ripped out his IV tubes and walked off into the desert to die. He also tends to set women on a pedestal, Peter confides, but it may be more complicated than idealization. Paul could walk out of a strip joint talking about paleolithic earth goddesses. It's as if he sees concealed within everyday people a deeper, ancient stratum of human life.

⚓ ⚓ ⚓

The cloud cover has returned, but at least we have good visibility. The weather, however, seems in transition. By afternoon the sun blazes brightly, and the sea has turned as smooth as a windless lake. You could see a fish jump from miles away. If there were any trees, the pollen would lie on the surface like yellow powder. The dead calm feels a little too eerie to enjoy fully, as if we will pay dearly later. Toward evening three lethargic grampus dolphins swim past, but otherwise the surface of the entire visible ocean resembles a single membrane.

Fortunately, this is an ideal time for the *Sea Shepherd II* to repair its newly broken water pump. I'm told that this particular malfunction has happened before. The *Sea Shepherd II* might be said to specialize in water-pump breakdowns. It will take at least several hours to fix, but the repairs should go faster—or at least easier—with the sea so quiet that the towrope floats listlessly on the surface. Everyone not immediately committed to the water pump savors a few moments of utter calm. A mild, mild day.

The pause and the good weather also mean that activity aboard the *Edward Abbey* again centers on film. The Brits from Yorkshire Television roam over the *Sea Shepherd II* getting background shots. Peter spends hours reviewing his footage in order to prepare some raw cuts for the television networks. In effect he's editing the film they will re-edit later, in a process that removes us still further from whatever event Peter observed and shaped by the choices he made in filming it. He also shoots fresh footage of Paul, in his photogenic captain's sweater, answering some newsy questions about the campaign. In an effort to get the shots he wants, Peter sometimes shouts his questions at Paul aggressively, like an opponent hurling insults. Right now he's shouting out his favorite provocation.

"What gives you the *right*?"

Actually, there is a clear answer to Peter's question, but it doesn't lend itself to sound bites. The 1982 UN World Charter for Nature—under principle 21, items (c) and (e)—includes the following legal language: "States and, to the extent that they are able, other public authorities, international organizations, individuals, groups, and corporations shall: ... (c) Implement the applicable international legal provisions for the conservation of nature and the protection of the environment... [and] (e) Safeguard and conserve nature in areas beyond national jurisdiction." Its language suggests that the UN World Charter for Nature just wasn't written for television.

Paul, at home around cameras, gazes coolly into the lens and fires back the short, punchy sound bites he knows Peter needs. He talks about our right to defend the planet against criminals who destroy it for their own profit and greed. Occasionally a colorful phrase like "bandit scum" grabs my attention. Mostly my mind wanders, however. I'm still trying to figure out how to defend the planet against every happy consumer who sprays a deodorant or buys a newspaper or drives a car.

Peter asks me to help out with the filming, as a kind of seafaring gofer. I'm grateful to do something besides stare at the glasslike surface of the North Pacific. Why be cynical about the artifice involved in filmmaking? Even though people think of documentary film as an objective record of truth, they aren't all wrong. Film has shaped us and our world. Moreover, writing, too, always shapes, edits and falsifies, no matter how hard writers struggle to put down what they regard as true. But then everybody knows that writing falls short of the truth. Every crew member on the *Edward Abbey* would write a different narrative of our journey, reshuffling details and viewing the events from different angles. Television, on the other hand, advertises its authenticity: the anchor stands on camera in the latest trouble spot, dressed in a jungle outfit, shirt open at the neck, dishing the facts. The pictures *are* the event. What you see is *real*.

We momentarily forget that camera crews record only what they have light and sound enough to get on tape. What about events that happen in the dark, out of earshot, beyond camera range, where almost everything really important goes on? Paul has no illusions about the manufactured images that television networks serve up in their competition for advertising dollars, nor about how such competitions shape and distort our understanding of the world.

"The nature of the mass media today," he claims, "is such that the truth is irrelevant. What is true and what is right to the general public is what is defined as true and right by the mass media."

He's not so much complaining as describing. If television is our chief definer of truth, then Paul will seek to use it in an effort at redefinition. As Peter squats, camera on his shoulder, shouting questions he's shouted fifty times before, Paul feeds back the answers—the two of them like a pair of NBA veterans trading passes on a fast break. With the cameras rolling, it's difficult after a while to tell what *isn't* performance.

"These are not fishermen," Paul says into the camera, disgust almost curling his lip. "They are businessmen out to maximize short-term profits by pillaging the natural resources of the sea."

I've heard it before, but I can't help admiring the delivery. With his movie-star tangle of silvery black hair, Paul looks the part, handsome, bluff, talking straight from the heart. Beneath the layers of repetition and artifice, who can say where the bedrock lies? Or is performance alone real in a culture where all the world's an electronic stage? My head feels a bit light. It's as if I were watching a sea captain do a perfect impersonation of a sea captain. A truth is being crafted with the carefully plotted, exact angle of deviation needed to gain entry into the mass media that define what we take to be true.

Meanwhile, repairs completed, the two ships travel into the twilight calm as if a mere towrope stretched across a tiny patch of ocean were the sign of a vast and deep connection.

CHAPTER SIX

DEAD OCEANS?

• • •

"Spiritually, the protection of the Earth is the most moral and just cause ever taken up in the history of the human species."

This is a sentence from a book Paul will publish soon entitled *Earthforce! The Art of Ecological Strategy*. He handed me a bound set of galley proofs after dinner, and I'll keep reading them as the campaign proceeds. I had no idea he was writing a book, and I'm pleased that, for whatever reason, he decided to share it with me. But mostly I'm pleased that I'm managing to hold down solid food, even if only soy milk and granola.

Meanwhile, I'm glimpsing bits of the plan. Or maybe it's less a plan than a procedure. We are heading due west, about eight knots per hour, a rate that may take us another week to reach the driftnet fishing grounds. The *Sea Shepherd II* recently installed a massive winch on the port side for confiscating nets. Peter feels certain we'll ram some ships. But no one is able to confirm whether Paul is planning to scuttle the *Sea Shepherd II*. There's one correct answer onboard to almost every question: "I just don't know."

It's disconcerting to know so little. Plans lend a sense of reassurance. They let you see if you're making progress. A moment ago, however, I read a passage in *Earthforce!* in which Paul describes the strategy of a sixteenth-century Japanese military theorist, Miyamoto Musashi. It's called "No Design, No Concept." If you don't make a plan, your opponents obvi-

Scamp keeps an eye on the troublesome towrope.

ously can't figure it out, so you always retain the advantage of surprise. Maybe a need to know the plan—or to *have* a plan—is an impediment to action, like an addiction to linear time.

The overcast sky makes a welcome change from yesterday's inert calm and blaze of sunshine. I'm almost glad to notice the sea grow rougher. A calm so total proves slightly unnerving, as if the world had suddenly died, and crew members still seem a little on edge. There's trouble with the towrope, which almost pulls Scamp over the bow in a possibly fatal fall. A little later, Paul, on the bridge, slips a Sam Kinison tape into the tape deck, but when he discovers it's heavy metal instead of comedy, he snaps the cartridge out abruptly. It seems at times that the human beings aboard these two ships crawling across the vast empty horizon of the North Pacific take their moods directly from the sky and sea.

⚓ ⚓ ⚓

Everyone, in a sense, lives on the fringes of the sea. No other planet in our solar system has an ocean. Life not only began in the oceans some 4 or 5 billion years ago. The human fetus still develops suspended in amniotic fluid that reproduces the chemical composition of seawater, and our blood duplicates the exact same life-giving ratio of water to salt. It's not surprising that we're so often drawn, if only for brief vacations, to the cliffs and beaches and ancient rhythms of the sea. Water covers nearly three-quarters of the globe. Even in the heart of the Midwest we stand surrounded by oceans on an island-continent ("Turtle Island," as some Indian tribes call North America).

Most people today, in fact, live directly beside an ocean. The majority of the earth's population inhabit coastal zones, and the percentage is expected to rise. The oceans, moreover, provide much of the world's food. The annual world catch of marine fish and shellfish has increased fourfold since 1950 to the level of 80 or 90 million tons, which reputable scientists think comes very near the upper limit of the oceanic food supply. A higher catch threatens to send fish populations into collapse.

Indeed, we no longer rely solely on the sea's natural supply. China, Japan and Australia now invest extensively in aquaculture—so-called fish farming and fish ranching—which supplies about 8 percent of the world's commercial fish harvest. But such new technologies may not be sufficient to hold off massive shortages. By the turn of the century, demand for marine fish and shellfish is expected to outstrip supply by some 20 percent.

Now—following conservative UN estimates—imagine once again that early in the next century the world population doubles. About two-thirds of this huge mass of 11 billion people will cluster in coastal zones. Will the seas still function as a dump for their sewage and industrial waste? Will the oceans still be able to provide them with food?

Commercial fishing, which today provides nearly all the world's oceanic products, has a history proving that humans are quite good at driving entire marine populations into collapse. Take, for example, whales. The explosive harpoon head, invented in 1864, permitted in far less than a century the destruction of massive numbers of sperm whales as humans extracted the oil for use in lamps, candles and cosmetics. When sperm whales nearly vanished, the harpooners turned to blue whales. When the blue whales grew scarce, they hunted fin whales, sei and minke whales, all of which declined precipitously. It was standard practice to hunt a species to the point of extinction.

The establishment of the International Whaling Commission in 1946 didn't signal a clear victory for the whales, despite full protection granted to humpback and blue whales in the 1960s. Whaling nations dominated the IWC, and the IWC aimed simply, in the language of economics, to safeguard whale stocks against overfishing and to provide for the optimal utilization of whale resources. *Overfishing* indicates the theoretical point at which a population declines faster than it can reproduce—a process that leads ultimately to collapse. In practice, overfishing may be impossible to detect until the damage is severe. Moreover, like some other important marine species, whales reproduce quite slowly, so overfishing, in combination with other recent hazards such as net entanglement and ship strikes, can devastate even large whale populations in a short time.

Only in 1982, under the influence of the nonwhaling nations recruited by Greenpeace, did the IWC declare a moratorium on commercial whaling, with a several-year delay in implementation. Even now, through a loophole in the IWC treaty, Japan, Iceland and Norway annually continue to take some three hundred whales each for so-called scientific purposes. Killing the whales, so goes their batty pretext, will help scientists explain why whales are in decline. Meanwhile the whale meat, salvaged after science has done its work, goes almost entirely to markets in Japan, where it sells today for about the price of Maine lobster in Manhattan.

The near extermination of various whale species offers merely one example of our ruthless practice on the high seas. Early explorers reported cod so numerous off the shores of North America that the fish were said to slow the ships. Sailors caught them by lowering baskets. Today the northern cod fisheries have nearly disappeared. In 1992 Newfoundland's small-boat cod fishery collapsed, costing twenty thousand jobs. The precipitous decline in stocks of pollack off Russia's Pacific coast has led Russia to demand a three-year moratorium on fishing. Along the 34,000-mile coast of Alaska, the commercial halibut season now opens and closes on the same day.

Overfishing, moreover, kills far more than just the target species. The incidental bycatch, as it is called, represents absolute waste, since regulations provide that nontarget species often cannot be landed. In 1991 ten thousand tons of North Pacific halibut were destroyed by fishermen targeting other species. Nor are fish the only loss. Recently, one official inspection of 133 halibut nets found, on average, six halibut per net—and seven seabirds. The waste and destruction mount rapidly. According to onboard monitors, during the course of just one trip spent fishing for squid, a fleet of thirty-two Japanese driftnet ships killed some twenty-two turtles, fifty-two fur seals, a thousand small cetaceans and more than fifty thousand sharks.

The pressure behind all this marine killing comes, of course, from the dinner table and pocketbook. The U.S. Marine Fisheries Service reports that the sudden popularity of "blackened redfish" in the 1980s nearly wiped out the red drum. It also reports that, in U.S. waters alone, 65 of the 153 species it assesses are currently overfished. According to the UN Food and Agriculture Organization, commercial fleets have experienced dramatically reduced catches since the 1970s among such staple species as Atlantic cod, Atlantic redfish, Atlantic mackerel, Northwest Atlantic herring and Western Pacific yellow croaker.

The situation worldwide is approaching economic and biological craziness. The *New York Times* notes that in 1989 the value of the worldwide catch reached a record $72 billion, while the cost of operating the world's 3 million fishing vessels soared well above that figure, to $92 billion. Meanwhile the technology for finding and catching fish improves each season. The largest trawl net, dragged through the ocean like a gigantic inflated sock, has an opening big enough to hold two stacks of Boeing 747 jet aircraft—six planes to a stack. Greenpeace claims that a trawl net some 30 percent larger is currently under construction.

The decline in fish stock parallels other alarming signs. The world's coral reefs—comparable to tropical rain forests in their biodiversity—now show serious damage from pollution, recreational activities and misguided engineering projects that increase the salinity of coastal waters. Toxin-producing plankton and killer red tides—sudden blooms of microscopic algae—are on the rise, matching the rise in human coastal populations whose sewage they consume.

A few round numbers collected by the UN suggest the scope of our ongoing assault on the oceans even if every fishing vessel were lying idle. Maritime pollution comes not only from the eight hundred thousand metric tons of municipal waste pumped into the sea every year. Shipping and dumping add another six hundred thousand metric tons of oil annually. Atmospheric pollution generated over land makes its way into the sea through rain and condensation, adding another three hundred thousand metric tons of pollutants, exactly matching the three hundred thousand metric tons generated as industrial waste. The higher math gets pretty frightening: over 2 million metric tons of human pollutants added to the oceans each year.

Is the ocean large enough to handle all this? In truth an ocean is made up of many distinctive ecosystems, and each oceanic ecosystem is an intricate network of interdependent biological species. When enough key species decline, or when new species suddenly take over, irreversible change occurs. The once teeming Grand Banks off Newfoundland, according to the *Halifax Chronicle-Herald*, is now a desert.

Although we hear and read about the "infinite" and "eternal" sea, the oceans, in fact, are neither timeless nor without bounds. For its first billion years, the earth's surface flowed with molten rock. The temperatures of the silicate fumes and toxic gases making up the lower atmosphere approached one thousand degrees centigrade. Like the air we breathe, the seashore is a much later invention.

Time really begins with the gradual cooling of the earth and the million-year rains that produced the ocean. Then, between 2 and 3 billion years ago, the first photosynthetic microorganisms suspended in these primeval seas produced the oxygen that life as we know it depends on. The point is this: life had its origin in the seas at a specific era, and the seas may well hold its terminal date as well. Can we rely on various national and international regulatory commissions to protect the oceans from a doubled world population? Worn-out rhetoric about the infinite, eternal sea functions today mainly as a self-delusive con job or cover-up, concealing an onslaught so ruinous that we now threaten to reduce three-quarters of the globe to a biological wasteland.

⚓ ⚓ ⚓

This afternoon our ship-to-shore radiophone brought some unexpected news. The Sea Shepherd Society of England has just declared war on Norway and Iceland because these two nations just dropped out of the International Whaling Commission and announced their intention to resume hunting whales.

The present moratorium on whaling may be imperfect, granted the catches allowed for "scientific" purposes, but it's far better than none. A resumption of whaling in defiance of widespread international protest represents a death sentence for the whales. When one country begins to hunt whales again, no matter how limited the catch, other countries will surely follow. New markets will open, encouraging illegal, unregulated suppliers. The decision by Norway and Iceland thus constitutes a call to action. There's talk among the crew that Paul may keep going after he hits the driftnetters and run the Northwest Passage before it freezes, surprising the Icelandic fleet and sinking it a second time. Crew members are already huddled in twos and threes deciding whether to sign on.

"In tactical decisions," I read just now in *Earthforce!*, "the most important factor is to conceal your plans."

Maybe there is really no plan. Or maybe Paul simply sets a general process in motion and lets the movement open up a series of possibilities for improvising. Even if a plan exists, on principle it must be impenetrably concealed, so that no one except Paul knows it. His rule for activists is not to trust anyone you haven't known for at least seven years. I do not assume that anything I have been told so far is accurate.

⚓ ⚓ ⚓

Paul has just gotten fresh information from the Sea Shepherd office in Santa Monica about the location of the North Pacific tuna boats, which usually fish somewhere near the driftnet fleets. We're still several days away, but closing steadily. It's a long, slow process. No wonder so few people have any firsthand knowledge of what is going on out here.

The facts about driftnet fishing are especially hard to come by. On December 20, 1991, the UN General Assembly passed Resolution 46/215, which requires that driftnet fishing on the high seas cease entirely by December 31, 1992. The original draft put the deadline six months earlier, but Japan engineered a loophole so it could continue driftnet fishing for another season. Japan, South Korea and Taiwan own the major fleets, and all three have agreed to comply with the UN ban. Agreeing to comply, however, is not identical with compliance. A 1992 article in the *Far Eastern Economic Review* states flatly, "The ban is being largely ignored by Taiwan's loosely regulated fishing industry."

A UN technical paper published in 1991 offers a grim picture of the driftnet menace. High-seas driftnet fisheries for squid alone involve more than seven hundred vessels and take over two hundred thousand tons of squid annually. An additional 130 driftnet vessels from Taiwan fish the Indian Ocean. Ships work for a month or two at a time, with the catch frozen on board. Catches per boat vary widely, as do the lengths of the various fishing seasons. In 1986 Korean vessels spent on average 175 days fishing, whereas Japanese vessels fished on average only 72 days. An accurate estimate of the total impact on the environment is impossible. The sober UN document concludes, however, that even crude indicators "do not encourage any idea that impacts may be minor."

Paul sees the driftnet fleets as engaged in a technological strip-mining of the oceans. It's a vicious circle. The high-tech commercial fishing methods deplete the stocks of fish, which means that corporations must invest more money in more sophisticated technology in order to extract enough fish from the depleted stocks to pay off the banks.

"The more fish they get," Paul says disgustedly, "the fewer fish there are. The fewer fish there are, the more elaborate the technology. They're not concerned about the future. They're only concerned about getting the maximum profit in the shortest period of time."

I ask him about changes in the oceans over the past twenty years, and he replies with a torrent of statistics.

"Salmon runs are down in Alaska, British Columbia, Washington. Shark populations have been reduced by about 60 percent. Marine mammals, seabirds and marine turtles have all been substantially reduced. So there's been a steady decline. It's estimated by the National Marine Fisheries Service that driftnets kill in excess of 1 million seabirds every year, which represents twenty-two species, of which thirteen are protected, threatened or endangered. And the incidental kill of marine mammals runs about a quarter of a million, and the fish they are taking are literally in the billions and billions. You're looking at about sixty thousand miles of driftnets used in the North Pacific. But it's a problem throughout the world. There's ten thousand kilometers in the Mediterranean, driftnetting in the Bay of Biscay, in the North Seas, in the Indian Ocean. So it's a global systematic assault on the biology of the oceans."

It's easy to forget that Paul, when he's not out on campaigns, spends some of his time lecturing at colleges and universities. Peter doesn't give lectures but tells me that a Japanese ship probably won't offer resistance. When Paul rammed a Japanese driftnet ship in 1990, inflicting some $2 million worth of damage, the official Japanese response was that nothing had happened. Publicity about their driftnet operations would hurt far more than a few million dollars' worth of lost equipment. Peter says the Taiwanese, on the other hand, are armed and dangerous. Nobody knows what to expect from the Koreans.

The idea of a trap seems quite reasonable. Don't these large fishing corporations expect another Sea Shepherd attack? I'm surprised they don't stock their ships with missile launchers, laser-guided rockets and antitank weapons from the international arms market. Who could say for sure what had happened out here if a couple of rickety Sea Shepherd ships went down?

⚓ ⚓ ⚓

"There's no point to civil disobedience," Paul says dryly, pursuing our earlier conversation. "You show up with your signs, the cops know you're coming, they arrest you, you post bail, get released, hire a lawyer and absolutely nothing changes. Civil disobedience now just plays into the system. It's like a game."

This is definitely no game. Driftnets are like nothing ever seen before in the ocean: curtains of death hanging six to ten feet below the surface. A single driftnet often extends some thirty-five miles! Nothing escapes it. Driftnets catch not only squid; they also intercept the salmon returning to spawn in American rivers, they kill dolphins and they strangle seabirds diving for squid caught in the invisible mesh. This deadly innovation resulted largely from the U.S. establishment in 1976 of a two-hundred-mile Exclusive Economic Zone vastly extending the previous three-mile limit on territorial waters. As other countries adopted similar laws, fishing nations had to shift their fleets from the continental shelves—now well inside the two-hundred-mile EEZ—to the open seas. Driftnets, which first appeared in 1978, were the answer.

Supposedly, then, the UN treaty against driftnet fishing will put an end to this destructive practice. But who's going to enforce the UN treaty? Who's going to stop countries from simply reflagging their vessels under the name of a nonsignatory nation? Japan says it will abide by the UN treaty—*after* the current fishing season—which allows plenty of time to reflag. Will Asian customers suddenly lose a taste for squid? Will no company find a way to supply a multimillion-dollar black market? Taiwan doesn't belong to the UN, and a February 1993 article in the *Far Eastern Economic Review* asserts that rogue trawlers originally from Taiwan may be dodging the official ban.

Certainly odd things can happen out in the North Pacific, a space as large as the continental United States. In May 1990 the Soviet Union arrested a fleet of twelve North Korean boats for illegal driftnet fishing close to the Kamchatka Peninsula. The Soviets discovered to their surprise that the North Korean boats were manned by a total of 169 Japanese fishermen. Eyewitnesses have informed Paul that South Korea is building a vast new fleet. The UN driftnet ban will undoubtedly be helpful, but driftnets are in one sense merely a symbol. Huge corporations looking for a quick return on investment will find new ways to vacuum the life out of the sea until, one day, there is little left worth fishing for.

The most striking change during the three decades he has been sailing out here, Paul says, is the absence of seabirds. No birds mean no fish. What will it be like twenty years from now? It's getting easier to understand why Paul thinks it will take a catastrophe to make people change their relation to the earth. He speaks bitterly of the 1992 UN Conference on Environment and Development (UNCED) at Rio, which was hamstrung by the Bush administration, who agreed to attend only at the last minute. The so-called Earth Summit, in Paul's view, amounted to nothing more than public relations—"a fiasco."

It's hard not to agree. The Preamble to UNCED's famous Agenda 21 begins by stating that humanity stands at a "defining moment in history." Agenda 21, however, at this defining historic moment, offers not a single binding resolution to alter our abuse of the oceans. Things haven't improved much in the UNCED follow-up sessions. At one recent meeting, which drew 150 diplomats along with lawyers, marine biologists and maritime industry officials, the participants agreed that many ocean species are being wiped out by overfishing. They almost totally disagreed, however, about where to assign blame or how to manage the remaining fish stocks.

Paul's frustration with the wrangling and posturing at Rio found a very personal focus when the Dalai Lama invited him to join a scheduled tour of a Greenpeace ship in port for the Earth Summit. Word must have slipped out. Just as Paul began to follow the Dalai Lama on board, two well-armed Brazilian soldiers blocked his way.

"You cannot come on board," the Greenpeace captain told Paul. "You are for violence. We are for peace."

"Some peace," Paul replied, "if it takes two guys with rifles to keep a guest of the Dalai Lama off your ship."

So, viewing the Earth Summit as a fiasco and the environmental movement as an illusion, Paul nonetheless persists in what he regards as the most moral and just struggle in the history of the human species. Ceaseless struggle has its costs, more than once wearing him down to exhaustion during protests mounted in subarctic temperatures, on tiny makeshift budgets, with constant draining logistics problems, against opponents incensed with hatred. It's no life for the irresolute. Little wonder that media analysts engage in a search for hidden motives. As Paul sees it, however, a search for motives ultimately leads back to the warrior's basic code of duty and allegiance.

"An Earth Warrior," he writes, "serves the biosphere."

He persists, then, despite all the difficulties, not because he seeks personal reward or even because he expects to prevail, but because duty and allegiance to the earth call him to protect marine wildlife, chiefly by enforcing laws, treaties and obligations that no one else will enforce. This may seem so hard to believe that assumptions about hidden motives remain the only alternative. Yet I have never met anyone like Paul who centers his allegiance and values on the interconnected community of life on earth—nonhuman as well as human—past, present and future. Such a person may require of us, among other hard changes, a new way of thinking about human motives.

Paul Watson, I'm finding, is more complex than I can grasp or convey. Self-confident, bawdy, laughing, full of stories drawn no doubt from his early years in the Canadian Coast Guard and Norwegian merchant marine, he feels at home in the toughest bars on at least three continents. A moment later, describing his run-ins with bureaucrats and police, he talks with an intelligence so quick and keen he could outmaneuver a hundred lawyers. A fast-thinking, legalistic mind proves useful in his line of work. The trick, when the police stop you, Paul explains, is to give the impression that you're a lawyer. Police tend to back off from hassling lawyers, he claims—on the basis of considerable experience.

His opponents may discover that his longshoreman's build is a cover for almost Zen-like perceptions. In a 1982 meeting with a group of Japanese tuna fishermen whose nets killed thousands of dolphins, Paul found the negotiations booby-trapped with the kinds of fruitless dilemmas that tie up professional logicians for centuries. If a fisherman and a dolphin were caught in a net, the Japanese repeatedly asked, which would Paul save? Paul declined to respond to the either/or gambit. He told the Japanese he had come to talk not about saving fishermen but about saving dolphins.

"They respected me for it," he says. "The Japanese understand duty."

Later, as we talk outside the galley, I find myself thinking that Paul sometimes sounds like a teacher or philosopher. Every fall, in fact, he teaches two courses at the Pasadena College of Art. He begins his course on Deep Ecology by posing a question worthy of the most slippery Japanese tuna fisherman.

"Which is more valuable?" he asks the students. "A Rembrandt engraving? The Sphinx? Or an endangered species such as the herring gull?"

Many people automatically assume that the Sphinx or the Rembrandt has the greatest value. Each day more than a hundred species go extinct—so why worry about one less species of seabird? Paul then notes how little time, from a geological point of view, has elapsed since the building of the Sphinx. He then asks the students how long it will take before a Rembrandt engraving crumbles into dust. The gulls, he points out, represent millions of years of evolutionary change. In other words, a million-year-old biological species is deemed perfectly expendable, while a three-hundred-year-old piece of paper commands a fortune on the art market. A human-centered outlook, he insists, stands behind not only our attitudes toward art and gulls but also our most commonplace judgments, acts and values.

In contrast to a human-centered or anthropocentric outlook, the revolutionary change in values that Paul endorses and embodies usually goes by the name *biocentrism.* A biocentric perspective rejects the view that the world exists for human purposes. It thus opposes the foundational text of Judeo-Christian scripture in which God gives Adam "dominion" over the birds and beasts. In biocentric thinking, no single species has dominion over the earth. The earth instead is viewed as a community where human and nonhuman life are intricately entwined, where all species live and develop together, where the biosphere, not humanity, occupies the center.

This change in outlook is as momentous and disorienting as the notorious paradigm shift from a Ptolemaic to a Copernican worldview. It requires us to rethink everything. For example, it underwrites a profoundly altered system of ethics. In *A Sand County Almanac* (1949), the revered naturalist Aldo Leopold offered a vision of the new values that flow from a biocentric perspective when he formulated his well-known "land ethic": "A thing is right when it tends to preserve the integrity, stability, and beauty of the biotic community. It is wrong when it tends otherwise."

Paul Watson, judging by Leopold's land ethic, would be securely in the right.

One of the most important things to grasp is that biocentrism puts the earth itself—not human knowledge *about* the earth—at the center. In an anthropocentric outlook, we inevitably separate ourselves from an object in order to know it. This is the classic method of science. Biocentrism, by contrast, assumes that we cannot separate ourselves from the earth and that, despite all our science, the earth is, in a fundamental sense, unknowable. It is unknowable not because we are ignorant but because it far exceeds in its complexity any system of thought that humans can scratch upon its surface, and thus its full truth will always elude our measurements and logic.

Biocentrism, moreover, is not such a weird or alien outlook. We all carry with us a biocentric heritage. *Homo sapiens* emerged in a world where human purposes lay far from the center, before the first cities appeared, before agriculture, before the inventions of madness, law and binary logic. We continue to experience the earth—both its beauties and terrors—in ways that completely outrun our capacity to understand it. Sunsets or newborn infants or storms at sea can move us with feelings too deep for thought. Whales, eagles, wolves, rivers and mountains all hold a portion of the earth's endless mystery. The earth, in a sense, recovers its sacredness as soon as it is released from the mindset that views it merely as raw materials, real estate or the stuff of human dominion. The biocentric experience of nature becomes a daily communion with realms beyond our knowledge, like a world where Wordsworth might hope to catch a glimpse of Proteus rising from the sea.

For Paul a biocentric perspective requires, at bottom, that we ask two specific questions concerning any human action: What is its impact on the planet? And what is its likely impact on future generations?

These questions are fundamental because a biocentric perspective means something very different to Paul than simply holding an opinion or belief, as if he were defending a proposition in a debate. A biocentric viewpoint colors how he thinks, feels and acts. It shapes his moment-to-moment experience of the world. Paul differs from most people not because he holds uncommon beliefs or occasionally rams ships but because he holds to an entire way of life in which the earth stands at the center. He gets up each morning in a very different relation to the planet than most people do, and this different relation influences such basic daily issues as how he earns his living, what things make him angry or happy and whom he trusts.

⚓ ⚓ ⚓

Ken Walker stands at the bow of the *Edward Abbey.*

The leaky water pump on the *Sea Shepherd II* again brings us to a stop—the third time the pump has needed repairs since we left Santa Cruz. The best way to deal with both the tedium and the anxiety, I've found, is to stop thinking about our goal. Or, maybe I'll just decide that I've embarked on the Sea Shepherd Diet Plan. You throw up for three days and thereafter live on soy milk and granola. I'm sure I've lost ten pounds. Peter says he always loses weight on these campaigns. The one time he came home unchanged, his wife wanted to know if he'd spent the time holed up in a San Francisco resort.

We've seen so little wildlife that, when we stop for repairs, I'm almost overjoyed to find the ship surrounded by thousands of small poisonous jellyfish called Portuguese men-of-war. These odd transparent, purplish creatures float on the waves and raise a semicircular membrane that catches the breeze like a sail, while just below the surface their ominous stringy tentacles hang down. Paul offers Trevor, his seventeen-year-old nephew aboard the *Sea Shepherd II,* $10 to kiss one, but Trevor for once declines a challenge.

The only other company in all this emptiness is our faithful albatross camped on the water. An albatross has a wingspan that must be five to eight feet. Especially when heading into the wind, it likes to hug the surface where the resistance is lowest, poised motionless above the water. It also likes to tip its long wings perpendicular to the surface, almost touching the waves in a graceful turn. My favorite maneuver, however, comes when swells turn the sea into long rolling valleys and hills. Gliding down into the valley, skimming along the surface of the water, the albatross completely disappears from view. Then minutes later it glides up again, suddenly and triumphantly, as if raised from the dead.

⚓ ⚓ ⚓

Peter says that Paul operates on these campaigns mostly by intuition. The campaigns take months of preparation, of course, but the preparations merely bring him to a point where the crucial move is intuitive. When the time comes, an Earth Warrior simply acts. This is what makes Paul Watson seem larger than life. He fills a room with his presence. You can't ignore him, forget him or mistake him for someone else. His bantering, ironic, argumentative talk is not just passing the time. It carries weight. Opinionated and provocative, but friendly too, sometimes almost gentle, he might be mistaken for a seagoing Paul Bunyan. Or antiBunyan. The mythology of commerce and anthropocentrism can't go much further than a colossal lumberjack who chops down entire forests and—a one-man earth-moving machine—gets credit for creating Puget Sound, the Black Hills and the Grand Canyon. It's not surprising that Paul Bunyan was introduced to a general audience in America, from 1914 to 1944, in pamphlets advertising the Red River Lumber Company.

Nor am I surprised to learn that Paul Watson once swam the thirty-two-mile Strait of Georgia between Vancouver Island and mainland Canada in protest against the annual Newfoundland seal hunt.

A born nomad, he seems to have traveled everywhere, from New Brunswick to Vancouver, from Wounded Knee to the seaports of Europe, from the Middle East to Africa and South America. He can launch into monologues on the history of ancient Rome or on the tribal divisions of modern Zimbabwe. He seems comfortable without a specific address. Moreover, he hasn't sold out. He holds no executive salary, no tax-free perks, no golden parachute. At forty-one, barefoot, dressed in cutoff black jeans and a tie-dyed T-shirt, he is out in the North Pacific once again to confront what he regards as crimes against the earth and its future generations. He can't worry if people choose not to notice or care what damage humans are doing to the planet. His biocentric outlook extends to a rejection of typical human-centered standards of measurement.

"Never be concerned with the idea of success or failure," he urges in *Earthforce!* "The Way of the Earth Warrior is to see things through."

CHAPTER SEVEN

MONKEYWRENCHES

• • •

While we stop for repairs, Paul pulls off his shirt and grabs a face mask, snorkel and a broad-bladed metal tool that looks like a giant putty knife. Then, still in his cutoffs, he dives repeatedly beneath the *Edward Abbey* to remove barnacles and algae. He slips through the water like a sea lion or dolphin, as if coming home. Stuart and Peter also take a quick dive overboard to cool off. Once they hit the water, they turn and swim back to the ladder so fast you can almost hear the ominous music from *Jaws*. They say the water is cold enough to suck out your breath. I'm at least one level below Peter and Stuart. I wouldn't jump into that freezing grey sea for all the apples in Eden.

Later the sun darts among the fast-gathering clouds overhead that stretch away in every direction. The sea has turned a little rougher again, but I'm learning to roll with its motion. What makes today the best and the worst day so far is that I finally got a call through to Ruth. Unfortunately, she's having as hard a time as I am. She worried a lot, not understanding why I hadn't called earlier, since Paul assured us that the radiophone would let us stay in touch. I used my new Walkman to tape Ruth's voice as it came over the speaker—not an intimate conversation, what with Paul, Peter and half the crew crowded around listening—but when I started to replay the tape, it was just too painful. Let it go. There's no need to increase my disquiet.

The important question aboard the *Edward Abbey* is not whether we have something (a radiophone, fresh water, a toilet, a lifeboat) but whether it *works*. So far our days at sea have been a continuous repair job. Today the automatic pilot joins the list of broken or disabled parts. Scamp, in another foul mood, spent all last night in an unsuccessful struggle with the water-purification system. Word just went out to all crew members that, in order to save water, from now on we piss off the back of the boat.

Pissing off the stern isn't as simple as it may sound, not at night, and especially not for the women. You walk back with the moon and stars as your guide, since a flashlight only gets in the way. The moist night air condenses on the metal deck and turns it ice-rink slick. The *Edward Abbey* rolls and sways as you grip for a foothold, leaning against the thin wire that separates you from the churning black ocean below. If you fall, nobody will hear the scream. Our staggered sleeping schedules mean that it may take days before anyone even *misses* you. A single wrong move—one unlucky lurch of the ship—and your shimmering stream of moonlit fluid will be your last.

⚓ ⚓ ⚓

The *Edward Abbey* takes its name from the late author of *The Monkeywrench Gang*. The 1976 novel, often called a cult classic, describes the adventures of four unlikely environmental saboteurs: a middle-aged doctor, a feminist nurse, a polygamous Mormon wilderness guide and a half-crazed Vietnam vet named George Washington Hayduke. They join forces to oppose the desecration of the natural landscape in the American West, with targets ranging from billboards and road-building equipment to a hydroelectric dam. Hayduke, for example, pours sand into the fuel tanks of huge earthmovers used to carve roads into the wilderness. He pulls up survey stakes, cuts electrical wires, derails trains.

This rowdy if high-principled crew carries on a protracted and colorful campaign of random eco-sabotage until the police finally catch them. The wild-eyed Hayduke appears to die in a blaze of gunfire, although he escapes unseen by diving off a steep cliff and floating away on the river below like an ineradicable lifeforce. His escape, completely improbable and deeply satisfying, offers a hope that nature still harbors a few anarchic spirits to protect it against the relentless onslaught of technology, development and government power. Paul quotes *The Monkeywrench Gang* in his book *Earthforce!:* "It is not enough to understand the natural world; the point is to defend it."

Paul knew Edward Abbey, and they seemed to understand each other pretty well. Abbey's last book ends with Hayduke making another improbable escape, amid another round of gunfire, when he swims out into the Sea of Cortez. There waiting to rescue him is Paul Watson with the *Sea Shepherd*.

Monkeywrenching, no small thanks to Edward Abbey, is the name that radical environmentalists give to the tactic of disrupting the industrial technology employed to degrade and destroy the earth. Its bible is the underground handbook *Ecodefense: A Field Guide to Monkeywrenching* (1985), edited, if that's the right word, by Dave Foreman, cofounder of the famous radical environmental group Earth First! Once a Washington lobbyist for the mainstream Wilderness Society, Foreman at last turned in his briefcase after watching both the government and the so-called environmentalists consistently sell out nature to the highest bidder.

In *Ecodefense* he provides helpful information about such Hayduke-like skills as putting abrasives into the lubricating system of earthmovers. He patiently explains how to jam locks with "liquid metal" glues, how to flatten tires with a "stiletto-type" knife, how to disable a tractor by opening the rain flap and pouring concrete down the exhaust pipe. Novices will learn the preferred method for burning down wooden billboards with the use of a homemade, low-tech, delayed combustion agent made from swimming pool cleaner and Score hair cream. No monkeywrench is too humble if it will increase corporate costs, diminish profits and slow down the relentless pace of industrial development.

Although Foreman and Earth First! are probably the best-known advocates of monkeywrenching, Rod Coronado and David Howitt, in sinking half the Icelandic whaling fleet, proved to be among its more literal practitioners, since they inflicted most of the damage with nothing more than a large, heavy tool. The monkeywrench painted on the side of the *Edward Abbey*—crossed with a painted tomahawk—offers a more complex meaning than, say, an anarchist's bomb. Any fool can destroy things or kill people. The monkeywrench and tomahawk—handheld, low-tech instruments borrowed from two quite different traditions—suggest that we already possess what we need to oppose the continuing rape of the planet. All we lack is a will to use the tools at hand.

Monkeywrenching can be dangerous, of course, but it is important to realize that monkeywrenchers always inflict damage on equipment, not people. Their ethic requires that they take great care to avoid injury to any living creature. As Foreman stresses, monkeywrenchers act deliberately and thoughtfully, with high seriousness, although he clearly finds deep joy and perhaps even a hell-raiser's intoxication in dismantling industrial machinery. He gives the impression that nobody ever accused him of turning down a six-pack. Monkeywrenchers aren't out to overthrow a social, political or economic system, he insists, but to defend the wilderness. "Even Republicans monkeywrench," he says engagingly.

There is one crucial difference, however, between Paul Watson and the Monkeywrench Gang. Edward Abbey's antiheroes, like Foreman and his cohorts, prefer to work in secret. The repeated maxim of *Ecodefense* is, Don't get caught! Infiltrators from the FBI and the Forest Service make it safest to work not just secretly but alone. Indeed the second edition of *Ecodefense* (1987) holds up well-known Earth First! insider Howie Wolke as a cautionary icon since he spent six months in jail after getting caught pulling up survey stakes along a proposed gas exploration road. ("Remember Howie Wolke!") Foreman and a handful of allies recently faced trial in Tucson on evidence supplied mainly by government informants, so the rule of secrecy now includes the maxim "Remember Dave Foreman!"

Paul Watson, by contrast, normally operates in the open. He knows that infiltrators sometimes join his crews, but he says he doesn't care, so long as they perform their shipboard duties. He keeps a careful watch for saboteurs, whose damage costs time and money. After all, he isn't in a good position to complain if his opponents succeed in sinking a Sea Shepherd vessel. Infiltrators, however, cannot be stopped. His defense is an openness so extreme that, paradoxically, it achieves a kind of absolute secrecy. By making his preparations completely public, he creates a situation in which an infiltrator has nothing new to learn.

As he demonstrated in Iceland, Paul at times not only doesn't avoid capture but insists on getting arrested. He may show up and demand that the authorities press charges. In this he most closely resembles the classic civil rights leaders. Like them, he openly breaks laws that he considers unjust, and thus his action is the opposite of lawless. He uses the law against the law in order to change the law.

Canada's Seal Protection Act, for example, made it a crime for anyone to come within eyesight of the annual seal hunt—by land, sea or air. This law obviously did not protect seals, which it allowed to be slaughtered, in secret, by the tens of thousands. It protected the rich families who ran the fur industry. Furthermore, the protection came at the cost of restricting the civil liberties of every other Canadian citizen. Paul chose not just to protest the law but to break it so ingeniously, flamboyantly and publicly that he almost forced the authorities to arrest him. His tactic thrust the seal hunt directly into the open. His case, in fact, went all the way to the Canadian Supreme Court, which in 1983 declared the Seal Protection Act unconstitutional.

Paul's monkeywrench tactics, then, are not vandalism, if by vandalism we mean random, senseless violence, but rather a calculated method employed for the specific ethical purpose of defending and preserving the earth. Of course most people oppose monkeywrenching, and environmental organizations often disavow it with special fervor, afraid that it will drain off support or turn potential allies into foes. Such fears don't influence Paul. What should you do if your government, illegally, declares it illegal to approach within a half-mile of the place where corporate-paid hunters smash the skulls of newborn seal pups? If you are Paul Watson, you do what it takes and don't worry about your critics.

⚓⚓⚓

Today, from my carefully rationed stock I allow myself a treat: clean underwear, clean socks and a clean T-shirt. Except for the dank, stained jeans that will have to last me another two weeks, I feel like a new man.

Well, almost. A high school football injury to my back flared up just as I began the book tour. This is old pain, returning at intervals for thirty-five years like a gully filled up by a sudden flood. Now I sit and stand up in slow motion. Every set of stairs on the *Edward Abbey* is a challenge. But I've also learned over the years how to deal with this obnoxious visitor.

Distraction helps, a recognized technique of pain management, and my discomfort begins to fade a little as I recall the endless tales about Jimmy—born Armando Kennedy, another given name that never makes it past the captain's log. Unlike such exotic figures as Fern the nudist cook, Jimmy still remains with the ship. Born in Mexico, dark and compact, with sullen good looks, he is apparently irresistible to many women. He also possesses one especially unusual trait: he is almost devoid of personal identity. While in Santa Cruz he lives like a hobo. In Key West he dates the daughter of the richest man on the island and dresses like a preppy. He meets a local family in a Panama bar, declares himself Panamanian and they take him home for the weekend. It goes without saying that when the Canadian Indians came on board to protest the anniversary voyage of the *Nina*, the *Pinta* and the *Santa Maria*, Jimmy turned Indian.

Such is Jimmy's apparent lack of internal structure that he holds no regular job aboard the *Sea Shepherd II*. Paul instead invents the unique class of "Jimmy duties," consisting of whatever Jimmy feels like doing. Thinking about a world where everyone is assigned only Jimmy duties provides me with a lot of distraction. Whatever the drawbacks to his fluid lifestyle, Jimmy has uncanny powers of adaptation that suggest a high probability of survival. Paul clearly just likes having him around. It occurs to me that if our ships ever go down, Jimmy may find himself swimming along with a school of fish and simply decide to turn salmon or tuna.

⚓ ⚓ ⚓

Perhaps it's Paul's lack of home ties that creates some of the sharpest differences between us. I grew up with loving parents and a close-knit family. The summer Sunday afternoons were spent under an old swamp maple in the backyard working through the *New York Times*, grilling steaks or staging birthdays (it's a big family). What did I have to flee or drift away from—except maybe upper middle-class feelings of privilege and disaffection? When Paul ran away to sea at sixteen, he was leaving behind both poverty and conflict. Now he doesn't own anything. He leases the Toyota and not only doesn't take a salary but won't even cut the grass.

"I used to have big arguments with my ex-wife on that one," he says, smiling, "because she would say I had to mow the lawn, and I would say, 'I'm not going to mow the lawn. I didn't want a lawn.' She said, 'Well, you've got to have a lawn.' I said, 'Why? I don't want a lawn! Throw some rocks out there.'"

"'The only reason I got this house,'" Paul continues after a pause, as if talking directly to his ex-wife, "'is because you wanted a house. So you got your house, and I ain't gonna mow the lawn!'"

It's sometimes tough to dig out the principles—if that's what they are—underlying Paul's stance on specific issues, such as his refusal to cut the grass. The worst mistake, however, is to assume that his views simply reproduce typical unexamined male bravado. Many of his responses, even if on occasion mixed with tough-guy bluster, connect with his core belief that an Earth Warrior's one true allegiance is to the earth. The problem with lawns, for example, isn't just that they need mowing but that, as he puts it, they're "antinature."

"Lawns are feudal estates," he goes on. "Putting one species anywhere and cultivating only one species is unnatural. It's much better to have a thousand different plants growing on your lawn."

For Paul a house and a lawn are more than just nuisances of suburban life, or small artificial slices of the planet to keep tidy. When we embrace them, paradoxically we simply continue to deepen our alienation from the earth. Fertilizer and rototillers have no necessary connection with the sense of an unknowable, infinitely diverse, millions of years–old web of life that stands behind our modern plastic parodies of nature: our pets, our chem-grow front yards, our indoor potted plants. The biosphere is where Paul hangs his hat.

"We come out of the earth," he says, "and we go back into the earth. I think you should be able to feel at home anywhere you are in the world."

Anywhere includes Los Angeles, which he counts as his home base when he's not out lecturing or on a campaign. And you won't hear him indulge in the facile pastime of L.A.-bashing.

"You know, to me it's a wasteland," he says, "but it's still part of the planet. I mean, the territory which is Los Angeles is just as sacred as the territory which is the Grand Canyon. It just happens to have man-made structures that are for the moment, you know, upon it. The pyramids will be gone in another ten thousand years. And what's twenty thousand years? That's nothing. They'll be dust blown away in the wind. And there isn't anything in the city of Los Angeles that's going to be there in ten thousand years."

He's probably right. It's disconcerting to talk with someone who actually lives his life by values implicit in gigantic blocks of time that to most people remain mere abstractions. His allegiance to the biosphere gives him an equally disconcerting view of space. Although Canadian-born, he favors the division of Canada into autonomous regions, including regions governed by the major Indian nations. States and countries strike him mostly as comical jigsaw pieces, redrawing their arbitrary boundaries every few generations. It's as if he looks at the earth with a satellite-eye vision.

But maybe his viewpoint owes less to satellites than to Native Americans. Paul may be, finally, most like the indigenous peoples who take a specific region for their homeland. They belong to tribes or nations, but they also view the entire planet as sacred and regard the rivers and animals as their kin: earth as mother, sky as father, the voices of grandfather spirits rolling in the thunder. While we carve up the world into patches of real estate fenced off with chain-link and mortgages, Paul, like the Indian, sees the land.

I feel more like Peter, who says he belongs to the tribe of white boys from Cape Cod.

⚓ ⚓ ⚓

Night is the time I like best aboard the *Edward Abbey*. Daylight somehow makes our isolation too visible. Everywhere I look is the evidence that we are alone out here. Each grey wave and rolling whitecap seems to express its indifference as to whether you live or die. Daylight shows too clearly the thin, sharp line which is all that separates you from nothingness. Night softens and erases the contrast as the moon moves among the dark clouds in pools of pale light. Night brings the warm campfire glow on the bridge where Paul keeps his watch. Night also blends the worlds above and below the sea. Far from the sunlit continental shelves where the rich undersea plant life creates a slow-motion landscape of coral and fern, out here the sea reaches straight down for two miles—so deep that sunlight cannot penetrate to the bottom. No plants survive in the total darkness on the open ocean floor. It is desert of thick silt and sediment deposited over millennia in a silent, slow descent of microscopic organisms. The teeth of sharks and the ear bones of whales mark the places where huge bodies once fell to rest and rotted in the silt. Sea creatures at these depths find their way by sound or feel. Eyes are as useless as colors. The brilliant bright red of the deep-sea shrimp looks jet-black down there.

Once in a while an angler pulls up an unknown creature out of this world of night. Fur seals, which feed far down in the sea, sometimes have bones in their stomachs that belong to no recognized fish. Never meant to see the light, such abyssal creatures often look so strange that they seem to be relics from an earlier geological era, like the long-necked, sawtoothed pliosaur, extinct since the Jurassic age, top carnivore in the prehistoric seas. Indeed, any creature that survives in the deepest ocean will likely perish at the surface, as if falling upward to die.

At night, however, the strangeness of the world below the surface doesn't seem quite so incomprehensible. It's what I see in the daytime that reminds me how vulnerable I am. So I look forward to the evening not for a sunset—the cloud-pack usually smothers the sun—but for the reassuring absences. The sunless canyons and stark, sea-swept plains two miles below seem as remote and placid as the rings of Saturn. The sea gives no hint of danger. I would do far better, in fact, if this entire campaign took place at night.

⚓ ⚓ ⚓

A low-pressure zone is moving toward us. We know about this thanks to the onboard weather fax that twice daily, when it's not malfunctioning, sends us small, nearly illegible maps printed on something like sandwich wrappers. Low pressure means more rough seas, but Paul hopes the worst chop will pass to the north and miss us. Peter thinks we'll reach the driftnet fishing grounds in about forty-eight hours, so these long days of preparation will soon give way to action. I'm unsure what to expect or how I'll react.

The secret for Paul, of course, is not to react but to act. The Earth Warrior, by acting, puts others in the position of having to react. The act of ramming their ships makes the driftnetters decide what to do next. Paul's emphasis on acting rather than reacting certainly gives him a degree of control. But he also understands how, in a sense, human control is fundamentally meaningless. He acts, that is, not so much against his opponents as *for* the earth. It is as if, through Paul, the earth, too, is acting—in ways and with consequences that no one can regulate.

Indeed, after reading further in *Earthforce!*, I now think I understand how Paul's calm and fearlessness might originate, as he suggests, in an earth-centered perspective. From a biocentric point of view, he is no longer an individual—a unique being with a name and a ship and a twelve-year-old daughter—but an almost anonymous participant in the vast, continuous cycles of nature: today in cutoffs, tomorrow as free-floating molecules shifting in the sunlight. The great advantage of human form is that for a time we become aware of our link to the earth and experience not just life itself but the conscious love of life. At this point, in Paul's view, we are almost by definition environmental activists.

"The love of life," he writes in *Earthforce!*, "inspires passion for life, which motivates the passionate defense of life. And, in a most ironic way, such passion for life allows the peaceful acceptance and understanding of the value your death has in the vibrant dance of the Continuum."

⚓ ⚓ ⚓

A half-smile crosses Paul's face as he responds to a question he's probably heard many times: Do his high-seas rammings constitute acts of piracy? "We're the good pirates," he says.

The good pirates of the Sea Shepherd Conservation Society were busy during the 1980s. The decade began with Paul serving a ten-day prison term in Quebec, a term that started, coincidentally, on the first day of the 1980 Newfoundland seal hunt. Although the conviction was later overturned, clearing his record, it didn't erase the time spent unjustly imprisoned, and it didn't help the seals. Meanwhile Sea Shepherd agents, enforcing the IWC quota on fin whales, sank the *Ibsa I* and *Ibsa II*, amounting to half the Spanish whaling fleet. Two weeks after a Sea Shepherd agent posted notices in the Canary Islands offering a $25,000 reward to anyone sinking the outlaw whaler *Astrid*, its owners retired the ship. So the whales did a little better than the seals in 1980.

But whales were still not doing well. The next year Paul landed with a crew in Siberia to document illegal whaling. In violation of IWC regulations, the Soviets were feeding whale meat to pen-raised minks and sables. A time-lapse film would show the whales ground up and slowly transformed into fur coats. As a Soviet destroyer and two helicopter gunships pursued the *Sea Shepherd II*, Paul refused their orders to halt, returning to U.S. waters with documentary evidence of the Soviet violations, which he gave to Congressman Don Bonkers for presentation to the IWC infractions committee.

Among the major victories of 1982, the *Sea Shepherd II* stopped in Hawaii en route to disrupt the notorious dolphin killing at Japanese-held Iki Island, where the local fishermen firmly but incorrectly believed that dolphins were ruining their catch. The Japanese consulate in Hawaii invited Paul to meet with a delegation of Iki Island fishermen. Under his threat of direct intervention, the fishermen agreed in writing to end the killing of dolphins. Later in the year, also after Sea Shepherd intervention, the government of Ireland agreed to shut down the grey seal hunt in the Irish Sea.

By 1983 it was clear that Paul Watson and the Sea Shepherd Conservation Society posed a threat to business as usual on the high seas. When Paul again interfered with the harp seal hunt in the Gulf of St. Lawrence, Canada sent two Coast Guard icebreakers, twenty helicopters and two hundred officers of the Royal Canadian Mounted Police to board and seize the *Sea Shepherd II*. In Quebec Paul was charged with violating the Seal Protection Act, given a twenty-one-month prison sentence and the *Sea Shepherd II* was confiscated. In April 1985, while free on appeal, Paul learned that the Supreme Court of Canada had ruled the Seal Protection Act unconstitutional. The government returned the *Sea Shepherd II* only after impounding it for almost two years and deliberately leaving it to rot.

In 1984, temporarily without a ship, Paul was drawn almost by default into a controversy surrounding Canada's government-funded wolf-kill in British Columbia. The instigator was a big-game hunter turned environment minister, Tony Brummett, who hatched a scheme with his ministry biologist to eliminate the few remaining wolves from the far north territories in order to provide more and bigger game for international trophy hunters. They planned to lure the wolves into the open with poison bait and then gun them down from helicopters. The scheme was not only grotesque commerce but also bad science. Wolves, though predators, kill mainly diseased, injured and aged animals, actually increasing the genetic health of the herds.

Brummett, obsessed with trophy elk and dollar signs, ignored the objections of scientists across Canada and continued with plans for the hunt. Left with almost no choice, Paul organized a band of protesters—under the leadership of his old pal from Wounded Knee, David Garrick—who traveled by plane and van to the remotest outpost in northern British Columbia. The temperatures at night dropped to thirty degrees below zero as Paul and the Project Wolf activists tramped into the wilderness. The obstacles created by subarctic conditions and hostile opponents led to a series of near-catastrophes, but, at the cost of death threats, exhaustion and frostbite, the Project Wolf team succeeded in focusing worldwide media attention on the protest and disrupting—though not stopping—the hunt.

With the decade not half over, in 1985, soon after Paul regained the *Sea Shepherd II,* he departed for the Danish-held Faeroe Islands. There he planned to document and disrupt the traditional slaughter of pilot whales, clubbed and hacked to death each year in the annual migration that takes them close to the Faeroes. The following year he returned with a BBC film crew. Despite encountering rifle fire and tear gas, Paul and the *Sea Shepherd II* successfully interfered with the slaughter while the BBC team documented the confrontation in an award-winning film entitled *Black Harvest.*

Anyone else might have been ready to retire. In 1987, however, Paul turned his attention to driftnet fishing in the North Pacific and the Bering Sea. In 1988 a Sea Shepherd agent documented the killing of dolphins by a U.S. tuna seiner, footage that contributed to the eventual ban on dolphin-kills by U.S. tuna companies. In 1989 the *Sea Shepherd II* intercepted two Venezuelan tuna seiners off Costa Rica, from which Paul, after a ten-hour standoff, succeeded in obtaining evidence of extensive dolphin-kills. Two weeks later, aided by information obtained from the Venezuelan ships, the *Sea Shepherd II* intercepted Mexican tuna seiners and disrupted their operations.

Finally, at the end of a busy decade, the good pirates in 1990 turned to the North Pacific in search of driftnet fleets. In August the *Sea Shepherd II* encountered a Japanese fleet north of Hawaii. Paul rammed two vessels and sank some thirty-five miles of driftnet. This confrontation was in effect the opening blow in the ongoing campaign I am now involved in.

Of course, the Sea Shepherd story could be told in greater detail, recounting the hard work and sacrifice of hundreds of volunteers, but ultimately what matters most is how such unsung, almost anonymous efforts help build up an overall decade-long record of commitment to protecting the environment. Acceptance of uncelebrated, unrewarded, often dangerous struggle—with no likelihood of ultimate success—is in part what it means to take up the role of Earth Warrior.

For some reason, Paul must find it very difficult to stay home and watch television.

⚓ ⚓ ⚓

We have fresh water! It's a murky yellow, and I'm not quite desperate enough to drink it, but at least we can boil it and occasionally flush the toilet. Scamp somehow bypassed the broken parts in the desalination system, which no doubt accounts for the clarity not being up to Perrier standards. Still, any improvement is encouraging. The winds have died down, the swells have evened out again and my mood has lightened. Hallelujah! Who cares that it's overcast and cold? After nine days at sea, I'm beginning to feel a bit more comfortable with the routine of unbroken crises. I sit outside at my normal writing post—the top step leading from the bridge to the aft deck—pen in hand, bundled up, thinking this is not such a bad place to be.

Hey! The albatross is back.

CHAPTER EIGHT

THE WINNIPEG WHORE

• • •

Eleven days at sea. We continue to creep along at a pace so slow it's like the nightmare in which you keep running and running and get nowhere. Still, this is the day Peter predicted we would meet up with the driftnetters. We start the morning at N 40° and W 150°. Let's see what happens.

The day begins, as I climb up from my cabin, with a domestic scene: Scamp and Chris alone on the bridge playing a hand of Skip-Bo, with the Indigo Girls on the tape deck. The bridge has a cozy feel, as four adults pretty much fill up the total space available for standing. Scamp and Chris have wedged themselves into a corner of the cramped tabletop that crosses the rear of the bridge, legs splayed out for support, cards tucked safely under their legs. It doesn't look comfortable, but at dawn the bridge offers almost a romantic solitude with the sea visible through the wide windshield and two narrow side doors. At normal hours a Coast Guard cutter is no place for private lives.

Everyone assumes that Scamp and Chris sleep together in the storage room behind the galley, where Chris set up a makeshift bunk atop a food locker, with a sheet hung up for privacy. Sea Shepherd romances are not uncommon. But it's no one's business and no one cares. They both work like horses. My entry is a signal for Scamp to unfold from his corner and check the engines. Closing the outer door, Chris reaches behind her for a worn copy of John Barth's hulking, postmodern remake of the eighteenth-century novel, *The Sot Weed Factor*.

"I usually read a lot of science fiction crap," she says, "so once in a while I try to work in one of the books you were supposed to read in school."

Chris, like Paul, is dyslexic. The authorities told her in the third grade that she'd never get out of remedial education, but here she is, a professional environmentalist, as she calls herself, with a college degree, sitting at the bridge of the *Edward Abbey* reading John Barth. Paul's dyslexia is severe enough that he still can't read certain words or remember how to loop a necktie. (The fashion in environmental protest, fortunately, tends toward open collars.) He says that he progressed from deckhand to able seaman without knowing how to tie a knot. Whenever a knot needed tying, he devised an excuse to do something else. His inventiveness in many other areas may owe something to dyslexia.

At breakfast Stuart takes a lot of ribbing about the special treatment he seems to give Jim. The jokes started several days ago with the birthday cake, after our drawn-out struggle to repair the desalinating system put everybody on edge, pushing the antagonism between Jim and Scamp right to the breaking point. Scamp chewed out Jim pretty fiercely just after Jim had spent almost the entire night at work on the water-purification problems. Probably to cheer him up and relieve a little tension, Stuart cooked Jim a special breakfast of hamburger and eggs. Now everybody checks out what Jim is eating.

Stuart returns the barbs with gusto. You can't disconcert someone who laughs at the gibe and then fires one back twice as comic and malicious. Without Stuart's quick wit, Jim mostly just smiles, a little embarrassed at the attention, maybe a little glad that everyone knows he gets special treatment. His ineffectual and vague replies, however, simply provide another source of barbed humor, not hostile exactly, but aggressive and at least a little mean-spirited. Peter jokes that the sixties were probably a great decade for Jim.

"While the rest of us were studying hard," he grins, "Jim must have been doing some really fabulous drugs."

Paul, not to be outdone when the conversation turns comic, weighs in with a Canadian story about the quick-thinking stockboy (Jim's antithesis and apparently a hero of Paul's) who unwisely mentions to his boss that everyone from Winnipeg is either a hockey player or a whore.

"My wife's from Winnipeg," snarls the boss.

"Is that so?" the kid replies. "What team does she play for?"

If we don't find some driftnet soon, I think we're all going to end up a bit loony. Instead we talk about the craziness we see onshore. About why American schoolchildren say a pledge of allegiance to the flag but Canadian children don't. About why Japan, with its tiny landmass, has millions of people playing golf. Chris tells us how Scamp, several years ago—having shown no previous interest in the environment—came to join up with the *Sea Shepherd II*. He was just hanging out in Norfolk, she says. When the *Sea Shepherd II* pulled into port he looked out his window and said, "Hey, a black ship! Cool!"

The seeping dementia isn't confined to the *Edward Abbey*. Word comes back via radio that the vegan women have led a revolt and taken control of the *Sea Shepherd II*. The conspirators must be Suniva Bronson, the beautiful cook given to long formless sweaters, whose light hair rings her face like an oval picture frame, and the dark-haired veteran radicals Myra and Sue, still in their twenties, who have sailed on Sea Shepherd campaigns since 1987. Apparently the three of them stormed the bridge and tied up the watch. Or so they claim.

"They could do it, too," says Peter.

⚓ ⚓ ⚓

Peter still thinks we'll find the bad guys, as he calls them, today. It might take a day longer—or possibly two—but everybody senses that we're close. It's taking me a long time to fall asleep at night, and I sleep lightly.

The combination of tension and boredom is unnerving. We've been traveling steadily for almost two weeks, about 180 miles each day, breakdowns included. The uniform seven-

or eight-mile-an-hour pace sometimes feels like we're standing still. Stuart says that this creeping tempo inflicts a kind of culture shock. You learn that the sea sets its own rules. If you try to hurry the sea, it will punish you. You break down, fall down, lurch, stumble, crash. So you go only as fast as the sea permits. The boredom got so heavy last night that most of the crew stayed up late playing poker for imaginary cash. The game ended when Peter cleared $30 million in one hand.

Still, every sense is on alert. Last night, even in my fitful sleep, I felt a change in the slap of the waves against the ship. Then the high-pitched, eerie hum of the propellers stopped. My bunk lies directly against the hull, so vibrations from the propellers pass along the metal and create a continuous two-note concert, like some minimalist New Age music. The tone rises and falls in time with our unchanging pace through the water, with no engine noise to interfere. Its otherworldly air has become reassuring. Even half-asleep, I know at once when the vibrations stop. The ship must have come to a halt. But so late at night? What's happening?

It's a good thing Meg was on watch because she kept us from crashing into the *Sea Shepherd II*. Their bridge simply forgot to inform us when Jon cut the engines for midnight repairs to the water pump, and our momentum almost crumpled us into their stern. When they don't make mistakes that risk a full-scale collision, Paul likes to poke fun at the vegan crew's inexperience and impulsiveness.

"They'll chase any light on the sea," he says. "Hell, last trip they chased the Trinidad-Tobago ferry."

Our midnight near-crash reminds me of the first rule of war articulated by maverick presidential candidate Ross Perot: Don't shoot yourself. Out here politics seems less real than the currents circulating below us in deep gyres the size of continents. My mind drifts again to the unknown species gliding through the blackness near the ocean floor, some radiating a strange phosphorescent glow. I can almost sense the ocean storing up heat during the day and moving great undersea masses of thermal energy northward from the tropics. Even though we left a presidential campaign in progress, the ocean overwhelms and obliterates it in the rhythms of the planet.

⚓ ⚓ ⚓

Laughter is important to Paul Watson. In the stereotypes of national humor, Canadians tend to be pictured as stolid and literal-minded people, not given to excess. ("What's a Canadian's favorite color? Grey. What's a Canadian's favorite flavor? Vanilla. How do you get ten Canadians out of a swimming pool? You ask them to get out of the pool.") Although stereotypes are as false as they are accurate, Paul must be a somewhat unusual Canadian. He claims that he's unusual simply in having been *born* Canadian—a reference to Canada's large immigrant population. Still, if Canadians have any claim to a solemn and serious manner, then Paul surely stands out for his laughter. Life on the *Edward Abbey* is not only not solemn, it's an intermittent but unending sequence of gags, jokes, pranks, comic remarks and horseplay. The horseplay today centers on Trevor, Paul's seventeen-year-old nephew.

He is long-haired, lanky and bright, but so restless that Paul wonders if he'll have the patience to finish high school. It's a serious impatience, for Trevor is also a committed radical activist who clearly reveres his uncle. His reverence, however, takes the form of regular, physical assaults. He feels driven to test himself against Paul, and this testing has gone on for years, usually in playful but bruising hand-to-hand combat. It all seems a little sick, with Trevor launching his attacks only to absorb punishment at a ratio approaching a hundred to one. Paul calls him a "pain pillow." Whatever its origin, uncle and nephew now live out the ambush-and-counterattack relationship I remember from Peter Sellers' films, where at any moment Inspector Clouseau is subject to attack by his faithful Asian manservant, Kato.

With the sea no longer so choppy but undulating again in slow gentle swells, the *Edward Abbey* approaches some twenty-five yards from the *Sea Shepherd II* to let the Brits send their cameras aboard for filming, and the two crews, now within shouting distance and eager for a break in routine, insult each other with good-natured taunts. Despite the TV cameras, Paul can't resist when he spots Trevor's unmistakable long skinny frame on the stern of the *Sea Shepherd II.* Relinquishing the wheel to Scamp, he disappears for a few minutes and emerges on the bridge armed with what I learn is a CO_2-powered paintball rifle.

Paintballs resemble marbles filled with colored dye. They are popular in war games in which U.S. corporations, in a questionable effort to teach teamwork, pay their executives to go off into the woods and shoot each other. Trevor, quickly understanding that he's the designated bull's-eye, embellishes his role with obscene gestures and lurid posturing. Within seconds Paul launches a rapid-fire series of paintballs, splattering the black stern of the *Sea Shepherd II* with brightly colored dye.

Trevor wins this round because the distance makes accurate shooting impossible, and Paul eventually gives up. The one direct hit comes a few minutes later when Meg borrows the paintball rifle and lobs a shot toward the nearly deserted stern of the *Sea Shepherd II,* where Mark—now two weeks past his senior thesis—stands idly watching the towrope. The single paintball hits him square on the cheekbone. Visibly upset, he thrusts his middle finger high in the air and turns his back, too proud to retreat. Dismayed and equally upset, Meg arranges to apologize to Mark over the radio. Such mishaps, however, aren't too unusual. Trevor, rigging a large, makeshift slingshot designed to assail his uncle with cabbages, tomatoes and whole heads of lettuce, manages only to shoot himself in the crotch.

Maybe laughter and seriousness for Paul aren't so much in oppostion as two sides of a coin. A solemn manner obviously befits a public figure speaking out against the degradation of the oceans. Could you smile about megacities like Boston and New York turning the ocean into an offshore sewage dump, about 90 percent of the U.S. swordfish containing mercury, about epidemic fibropapillomas killing sea turtles with baseball-sized tumors? In the face of such knowledge, Paul's humor and horseplay must help sustain the balancing act that keeps him from turning into a one-dimensional zealot. Despite his invaluable work as a consumer advocate, Ralph Nader always looks to me like a somber one-track man who has forgotten—or never known—the pleasures of life, even such dumb pleasures as paintball guns.

Paul's rapid swings from jokes to seriousness make him very unpredictable. Then, of course, both moods can quickly give way to a calm so emotionless it is deeply perplexing. It's not the calm of relaxation or self-control but, apparently, of utter emptiness or total absorption. His voice, as if wholly distanced from the claim of social ties, falls into a clipped, inexpressive monotone. Whatever its source, such composure must be useful for someone who needs to keep cool under fire. Perhaps it's a kind of superlow gear, or a blankness that also serves to wipe out panic. Paul clearly doesn't care if people find him hard to understand. An unpredictable and impenetrable character may prove an advantage in a warrior, an internal equivalent to the "plan of no plan."

The joking sometimes goes beyond horseplay to expose a bitter, satiric, scornful edge. Like other products of Catholic education, Paul seems to take great relish in skewering his teachers, poking holes in their doctrine and abusing their faith, although in fairness he criticizes almost every major world religion as equally anthropocentric, irrational and unnatural. His half-serious invective against various theological practices sounds like something cooked up by a composite of Voltaire, Darwin and Lenny Bruce.

Paul's arguments often include an element that suggests someone who is fundamentally self-taught. In academic settings I've never encountered anything like his regular cascade of dates and details. Academics usually talk as if God had decreed that conversation must never descend to specifics. The worst possible breach of academic etiquette is, in mixed company, to cite a verifiable fact. Paul's conversation, by contrast, overflows with obscure tidbits about third-century popes, ancient climate or the grains that Roman soldiers carried in their saddlebags. Often the details provide a groundwork for elaborate theories. Saul's conversion on the road to Damascus results from the hallucinogenic properties of rye mold. Beginning with Adam, whose name in Sumerian means "red clay," the Book of Genesis recounts an allegory of environmental change. When Cain, whose name associates him with farmers, slays his nomadic brother Abel, he acts out the epochal shift ten thousand years ago when city-based, agricultural civilizations nearly exterminated the wandering hunter-gatherer tribes who preceded them.

No matter that biblical etymologies are hotly disputed. It's a plausible, irreverent, useful version, this "eco-deconstruction," and I'm sure he never heard it from the nuns.

Laughter for Paul seems connected ultimately with liberation. He likes outrageousness and sacrilege, which may explain not just his free hand with scripture but also his fondness for inventive, obscene, iconoclastic comedians like George Carlin. Over the ship's radio he challenges the *Sea Shepherd II* bridge to a riddle-telling contest, choosing to lead off with one he knows will offend their vegan, feminist and animal-rights sensibilities.

"What's the difference between meat and fish?" [Pause.] "You can't beat your fish."

A male voice from the *Sea Shepherd II* promises a suitably indecent riddle in reply, but then an embarrassed silence follows. We conjecture that one of the women on the *Sea Shepherd II* has just wandered onto the bridge and put a halt to the puero-macho war of wits.

"The great thing about being out here," says Paul, gesturing at the unblocked horizon stretching in every direction, "is the freedom. Nobody has any authority over you."

⚓ ⚓ ⚓

This morning Scamp's handwritten notice—composed with almost academic tact—appears above the ship's one working toilet: "Absolutely no paper in the head. Deposit only what you pass."

Soiled toilet paper from now on goes into a small, round canister strapped with bungee cords to the pipes beneath the sink. It has a lid, but the arrangement doesn't encourage you to linger.

Now Scamp emerges from the galley with a terse update: "Don't use the toilets at all."

Apparently the repairs to the water-purification system need additional work, because once again we're almost out of fresh water. Still we plunge on. Today it feels as if we're covering more miles side to side than straight ahead. Readjusting his estimate, Peter now thinks we will need a couple of days more to reach the driftnet grounds. I'm silently debating whether, when the action starts, to shift with Paul to the *Sea Shepherd II* or to stay with Peter on the *Edward Abbey*. Peter is less likely to get us killed, and my instinct says to stay put. Or is it just faintheartedness?

⚓ ⚓ ⚓

Stuart and Jim make a strange addition to the crew of the *Edward Abbey*. A born organizer, skilled in management and superefficient, Stuart now finds himself unemployed in the middle of a recession. Although he walked away from the swank consumer world of Rodeo Drive, it isn't clear where he's going. Job interviews by the dozen still haven't produced an offer, while his first two semesters at an unaccredited law school have proved so expensive that he's not sure he'll continue. After fourteen years of sixty-hour weeks managing someone else's business, he shows the classic signs of burnout and midlife crisis. He recently leased a new Corvette, although he knows he can't keep up the payments. He has one month's rent left in the bank. When Mark called from the Sea Shepherd office two days before departure to offer him an unpaid job as cook, Stuart packed his bags. He says he doesn't know what comes next, but he does know that for the first time he's doing what he wants.

With his pale good looks and trim mustache, Jim appears far more vulnerable than Stuart, even fragile, despite the strong, lean body of a shipyard welder. I like him and admire him for being here, but his omnipresent dark glasses seem to hide something, maybe deep insecurities or a puzzled rage, as if he can't quite understand why his idealism and good intentions tend to evoke hostility. He has an argumentative streak, not easily held under control, that turns absolutely passionate when he defends Jimmy Carter as a moral leader. Blood flushes his cheeks as he debates with Paul, who takes the opposite position—that Carter should have given Iran a twenty-four-hour ultimatum to return its American hostages or America would level its cities.

"The Iranians respect power," Paul says calmly. "They'd return the hostages."

Jim is no match for Paul in argument and doesn't possess Stuart's gift for defusing confrontations. While Stuart is funny and engaging, with a strong sense of independence and easy-going self-confidence tempered by genuine southern courtesy, Jim seems uncertain and easily upset. Sometimes, I suspect, he alters his views slightly to please the person he's talking with, but moments later he can be rigid and unyielding. In defending Jimmy Carter he may be indirectly sticking up for himself, an underdog, an outsider, someone whose strict moral code isolates him from less scrupulous people.

Paul, at any rate, can't be defeated in conversation—so Jim is in good company. In *Earthforce!* Paul cautions that the Earth Warrior, in facing opponents or the media, must always seem in control and never at a loss for an answer. If you don't know the facts, he advises, follow the example of President Ronald Reagan and just make them up.

⚓ ⚓ ⚓

At 6:10 p.m. we spot a group of four humpback whales. At first there are only indistinct plumes of spray, but then the spray draws closer and we can make out the enormous tails rising and slowly folding back. Everyone runs to starboard and watches silently until the huge mammals disappear in the distance, as if we've just encountered visitors from another world—which, in a sense, we have.

Jim Knapp pauses outside the engine room.

It is Paul who knew that the tails and rolling bodies meant humpbacks. Sam, on the *Sea Shepherd II* radio, tells us they were blue whales, but Paul says that blues prefer colder latitudes. It's thanks to him and other environmentalists that some whale species have survived at all. Commercial whaling has greatly reduced humpback populations, and blue whales have been severely depleted. In fact, as few as 660 Antarctic blue whales remain from a population once in the hundreds of thousands. Despite sixty years of protection, the northern right whale has dwindled to a few hundred animals.

Paul says his turning point came when he looked deep into the eye of a dying whale. Steering his zodiac close beside two hunted whales, he was trying to stay between the whales and the harpoon cannon mounted on a massive Russian whaling ship. He could see the gunner poised to fire. It was perilous work—not getting swamped by the Russian ship or smashed by the whales, staying close enough that the gunner couldn't shoot without hitting him. He could feel the pulse of the engines and the panic of the whales. Suddenly a huge rolling wave sent the zodiac into a trough, and the harpooner shot over the top, hitting one of the whales and showering the zodiac with blood.

Experienced harpooners shoot the female first because the male, rather than diving, will stay to defend his mate. Amid the screams of the dying female, the male turned to attack the whaling ship. Its path headed straight through the tiny zodiac.

Paul says it looked like certain death. The enraged whale drove through the sea directly toward him, thousands of pounds churning the bloody water. There was nothing Paul could do to keep from being crushed. At the last second, the whale arched above the frail zodiac, barely missing it. Paul looked directly into an eye about as large as a human fist—a miraculous extended moment, an epiphany—in mute communion with another species. As he gazed into that huge eye, he realized the whale understood he meant to help. Then the cannon fired again, and this time the male, too, rolled and screamed in a torrent of blood.

Peter, working side by side with him almost every day, regards Paul as unique. "You may like him or hate him," he says, "but you can't deny he's been out here doing it, putting his life on the line longer than almost anyone else in the environmental movement. And he's still doing it. He could have retired long ago as an elder statesman, taken a cushy job with some wildlife foundation. But here he is."

⚓ ⚓ ⚓

There's one part of Paul that makes me uneasy—and it's not the redneck crudeness he sometimes deliberately affects, often because he enjoys shocking people or because he hates pieties and hero-worship. Yesterday he spent about an hour on the bridge cleaning and test-firing two Civil War pistols. A Civil War cannon, covered with canvas but still quite usable, points out over the stern. Recently the directors of the Sea Shepherd Conservation Society split (three votes against two) over whether the *Sea Shepherd II* should carry firearms. One director argued that if the ship carried weapons, it would someday use them.

"Hell," Paul replied, "we've been carrying weapons for ten years now and never used them."

As captain he has sole responsibility for the lives of his crew. Fifteen hundred miles from land, he says, you never know who might try to board your ship. His argument has some weight: isolation out here is absolute.

"What am I supposed to do?" he asks in exasperation. "Call 911?"

My relation to weapons—even guns intended solely for self-defense—is wary and distrustful. My mother was accidentally shot by her brother when they were kids—the round scar on her thigh is proof—so I grew up without the usual quota of plastic firearms. And hunting, even if it expresses a warped love for nature, has always struck me as brutal and absurd. Our ancestors hunted and hunters play a role in modern wildlife management—after all, grocery stores don't rely on suicidal livestock.

Paul Watson explains the workings of the Civil War cannon on the *Edward Abbey*.

But the argument that hunters eat what they kill does not impress me. Why not change your diet? Why not stuff a cow's head for the den? Some people just take pleasure in killing animals.

So I acknowledge that I come to guns with built-in ignorance, prejudice and with no responsibility for the lives of a crew. The acknowledgment doesn't help.

Paul is simply comfortable with guns. Perhaps, as Bob Hunter proposes in his book *Warriors of the Rainbow,* Paul has something of a militaristic streak. Given our mission and the chance we may find guns lined up against us, it's probably good that he knows his way around weapons. But it's also reassuring to find the following passage in*Earthforce!:* "DO NOT GET YOURSELF OR YOUR FOLLOWERS AND ALLIES KILLED OR INJURED. You or your followers will be of little use to the Earth if hospitalized, maimed, or in a grave."

Still, force begets force, and you can't always control the counterviolence. Paul's life has been threatened many times, and his opponents do not restrict themselves to threats. Peter quips that in public he always stands a couple of steps behind Paul—and it's not entirely a joke. I sense that Paul doesn't intend to retreat if a driftnet ship responds with violence, and he's very well prepared to defend himself, with guns if necessary.

A dozen years in the classroom have made me a believer in peaceful tactics, such as dialogue. But I'm kidding myself, too. Dialogue can be a ruse or a dead-end, dragging on endlessly or just breaking down. Civil disobedience and peaceful protest can be deliberately used to provoke a violent response. Nonviolent organizers may even *count on* the publicity that violent responses bring. Finally, cleaning and test-firing Civil War pistols does not constitute an act of violence. It's not illegal to own a Civil War cannon. Worst of all for someone who dislikes self-contradiction, I'm no pacifist. I believe in fighting back when attacked, and I'll push hard for what I believe in. The question of guns and violence has got me in a terrible muddle, and the muddle, as much as the violence, may be what makes me so uneasy.

⚓ ⚓ ⚓

Last night Paul was reading aloud from anthropologist Carlos Castaneda's *Tales of Power,* where the Yaqui Indian sorcerer Don Juan explains why the life of the warrior cannot be, as some people imagine, cold and lonely. The warrior, he says, takes the earth for his beloved and thus, wherever he goes, he is never alone. I suspect that Paul applies Castaneda's words to his own life. He appears to be immune from loneliness and professes to be baffled why the Americans onboard—and I'm the chief offender—keep phoning their wives and girlfriends. It's not just that Paul, currently divorced and unattached, thinks of the earth as his beloved. There could be an unwarriorlike boundary issue at play. Canadian men, he seems to imply, are made of sterner stuff.

The radiophone calls are a disconcerting ritual because they take place more or less in public, like a sideshow. No one would miss it. First the radio room fills with spectators, and then, after the long wait for a connection, you talk into a microphone and the reply is broadcast over the speaker. The audience can expect to be rewarded with the unintentional comedy of lines like "I love you. Over." As every ship in the North Pacific can hear what Ruth says, including the Coast Guard, we don't get too intimate, and we never mention details of the campaign. Ham radio operators seem to have no problem tracking our whereabouts, and they, too, are probably glued to their speakers. I've begun to wonder who *isn't* listening in. It doesn't matter. The phone calls to Ruth are a lifeline that keeps me going, and I no longer care who overhears.

CHAPTER NINE

SQUID

• • •

After days of punching laboriously through the North Pacific, the tension continues to grow as we push closer to the fishing grounds. But not for Paul. This morning he's standing near the open door of the bridge repairing the two Civil War pistols that started to give him trouble yesterday. Finally satisfied, he puts his arm out the side door. I hear rapid metallic clicks as he pulls the trigger repeatedly, but the pistols continue to misfire and the clicking increases. Then, at random, a sudden incredible blast almost lifts me off my feet.

A hundred years ago, these pistols probably killed someone. Paul is aiming at a cardboard box floating some twenty yards off the starboard side, but the round, soft lead bullets and the untooled barrels make shooting very inaccurate. These pistols would guarantee a kill only if you placed the barrel right against a person's chest. The Civil War must have been an intimate affair. The blast from Paul's one lone shot sends shockwaves right down into my bones. Of course a soldier, eyeball to eyeball with an enemy, would like to feel confident that his pistol wouldn't misfire. How many men died when they pulled the trigger and nothing happened? As Paul's single shattering blast begins to fade, I hear maybe ten or twenty clusters of repeated, frustrated clicks.

Swearing softly as he disassembles the capricious pistols, Paul says that it's possible the Japanese are tracking us by satellite, moving as we move, staying always just out of reach. Aboard the *Edward Abbey* our most sophisticated instruments for gathering intelligence are an aged radar screen, worn down to a mere five-mile range, and a weather fax with a mind of its own. According to Peter, however, maps and radar don't matter much as Paul searches for his quarry. One day he gets up, decides to change course and suddenly there they are.

⚓ ⚓ ⚓

The weather may be fine—a ring of white clouds circling the horizon and blue sky overhead—but the sea has turned so choppy that Peter was tossed out of his bunk last night. I awoke a little earlier than usual, before dawn. I felt tired, tired of pitching all night on my inch-thick raw foam slab, tired of no showers, tired of hair so matted and tangled that a comb is useless, tired of pissing off the back of the boat. Although a high-pressure zone keeps the weather cool and sunny, these chopping whitecaps pushed down relentlessly from the Bering Sea make life very difficult. A familiar queasy feeling begins to start up in my lower abdomen.

"Get used to it," Ken advises as I do my two-handed monkey walk (never let go of a support) back toward the stern. "Probably this is about as good as it gets from now on."

At least nobody's driving a bulldozer at my head or setting police dogs on me. There are worse ways to mount a protest. I return to my bunk, push aside the wadded sleeping bag, swallow a Dramamine tablet and doze for a few hours. No one else seems to be moving either.

Later, free from the blues, I sit on my familiar open-air perch—the top of the three stairs leading from the galley to the bridge—and try to recall some numbers. The Sea Shepherd Conservation Society: small, with some twenty thousand members contributing its entire annual budget of about $500,000, a modest sum compared, say, to 1992 revenue around $275 million for The Nature Conservancy. Paul accomplishes a lot with little money. A weak joke begins to form in my brain about more bang for your buck, but I give up. More important today, numbers have a crisp, reassuring definiteness, a relief from all the unknowns and conjectures that surround this campaign.

A raggedness is spreading throughout the crew as we lurch on our decommissioned roller coaster. Take Chris's bandaged hand. Above the bunk she rigged in the storage room, a hatch in the ceiling opens onto the aft deck. The hatch resembles a circular steel trapdoor weighing about fifty pounds, and it closes around a raised metal flange that protrudes from the deck, creating a watertight seal. Chris ordinarily keeps the hatch raised for ventilation, so last night she awoke to a soft rain falling through the circular hole directly above her bunk. Wet and frustrated, she clambered up the short metal ladder to close it, and as she groped in the dark, steadying herself by holding onto the circular flange, the hatch suddenly collapsed and fell across her fingers.

She's lucky it didn't cut them off. Lucky too, she says, that she has a high tolerance for pain. I wince to see her move around the ship—now pitching badly—with her bandaged hand held up beside her shoulder. We're a long way from a hospital.

After lunch a talkative foursome—Paul, Stuart, Jim and I—linger in the galley discussing environmental issues. I'm pleased to find that Paul and I agree on basics. For Paul, too, the problem starts with population. The mathematics of 5.6 billion people means that each day generates *x* times 5.6 billion decisions about what to consume: food, firewood, electric power, boats, microwaves, Winnebagos. Each decision, perhaps innocent enough, contributes to a massive cumulative impact. Then, of course, all the stuff we consume eventually gets disposed of. Our dumps and sewers and landfills just can't handle the overload.

The developed world is lucky, in a grim sort of way, that 20 percent of the earth's population lives on less than $1 per day.

It means they can't buy cars, microwaves and Winnebagos, which indirectly helps control pollution. Poverty, however, correlates directly with escalating population growth. Poor people use the cheapest and dirtiest fuels. When global population doubles to 11 billion, we'd better hope that presently underdeveloped countries have eliminated poverty and learned how to sustain economic growth without repeating the history of massive environmental degradation in the developed world. Any improvement in the West could be completely offset by what happens in China, India and Africa.

Paul believes that corporations and governments deserve a big share of the blame. Suppose that individuals everywhere, in a burst of enlightenment, decide to limit their families and cut back consumption. Will CEOs and government bureaucrats base their decisions on what improves the long-term health of the earth? Here's a test case: The developed world today produces tons of radioactive nuclear waste that will remain lethal long after its containers molder into dust. Nobody knows how to build containers that outlast radioactive plutonium. How many researchers in government, corporations or private think tanks are working on the problem of protecting people ten thousand years in the future from our legacy of nuclear waste?

Paul has a less global question he likes to ask his students at the Pasadena College of Art: How many can name their great-grandparents?

Try it. Surprisingly few people know the names of their great-grandparents, let alone any details about them. This amnesia is unique to modern developed nations. Today Bedouin clansmen in Egypt, living as their ancestors did in a harsh desert, can recite ten to fourteen generations through the male line. Our forgetting, or just plain not bothering to learn, reflects a culturewide lack of interest in our own immediate ancestors.

The point of Paul's question is this: If we attribute so little importance to our own immediate family members, who lived just a few decades ago, how can we expect anyone to make provision for people alive two hundred years from now? The Iroquois, by contrast, had a rule that no tribe can make a decision without considering its impact on the next seven generations.

It's easy to see why Paul comes to a pessimistic assessment of the future, but it's quite admirable that he doesn't let pessimism force him into despair or paralysis. He lives as a warrior, serving the earth, as he's done for the past twenty-five years. His methods are certainly controversial and imperfect. But should he opt for a tie and briefcase, quietly waiting in line until lobbyists and bureaucrats with their private agendas at last propose the ideal compromise? Should he do nothing until someone discovers a perfect tactic that offends nobody? Someone once asked him accusingly if the *Sea Shepherd II,* which burns tons of diesel fuel, doesn't cause air pollution.

"Yeah," Paul replied, "but I can't ram driftnet ships with a sailboat."

⚓ ⚓ ⚓

At about 10:00 A.M. Paul swings us 90 degrees north, in the direction of the Bay of Alaska. The Sea Shepherd office has just radioed new coordinates for the driftnet fleet. Although the information has almost no chance of being accurate, it's all we've got. Meanwhile we learn that Hurricane David has just hit Baja California, and is moving north. It won't strike us directly, Paul figures, but we might get some high seas as a byproduct. Ever since we turned north the *Edward Abbey* has been pitching and rocking again. Hold on.

Ken and I, braced against the choppy seas, chat by the zodiac on the aft deck, grateful for some fresh air. He's on a break from the engine room, his pony tail and open high-tops giving him the look of a kid just off the playground. He's easy to find hanging out around the zodiac because he's the only crew member with a two-pack-a-day cigarette habit. He must know engines; he claims he's never been out of work for more than a week. Like Jim, his heart lies in the Northwest, especially

Oregon, so he doesn't really mind walking off his latest job in southern California.

"Turn right, it's L.A. Turn left, it's San Diego," he says disgustedly. "One big fuckin' industrial waste."

Talking with Ken is always reassuring because it's hard to imagine someone more stable and grounded. His favorite topic of conversation is his golden retriever, whom I'm beginning to know pretty well. Talking with Ken also helps me learn something about my fear. It comes and goes, but it always comes back. It tells me that I have led a sheltered life, pushing around little blips of light on a computer screen, but it also tells me that, like Ken, I'm a born land animal. I like the feel of the earth firm beneath my feet.

These are not blinding revelations ripped from the depths of the soul, but maybe they are useful. A person's likes and dislikes constitute a set of limitations, which suggests why it is good to detect and confront them. Perhaps they're what Paul refers to when he writes in *Earthforce!* that we are locked into our sufferings, and our pleasures are the seal.

We can struggle against our limitations, of course, and make them a little less constraining, but it also makes sense to acknowledge and accept them, much as Paul has come to acknowledge and accept his own death. In accepting them, we may also come to pass through or beyond them. I need to own up to my fear, really experience it, come to taste and smell it, even see it as a life force, learning at last what its value or liability is. It's certain, however, that whatever I do to help protect the environment from now on, I will do on land.

⚓ ⚓ ⚓

The driftnet ships look mostly for squid, which must be one of nature's homeliest creatures. A common garden slug can count on more admirers. Long and narrow, squid have ten snaky arms at one end. Two of the arms, longer than the others, are tentacles that snare prey, while the other eight hold the prey firmly in place for the parrotlike beak. For such primitive-looking beasts, squid have an unusually complex nervous system. Cells in the skin produce bioluminescence; other cells allow the squid to change color swiftly, to turn red, pink, brown, blue or pale green-gold speckled with black. Scientists don't know whether the changes in color are a complex communication system or just a form of camouflage. Stretched out and in motion, the squid resembles a long, thick, fleshy fountain pen, with the tentacles in front forming a brushlike tip. About where the barrel narrows at the nib, two immense bulbous eyes stare out, nearly as keen and complex as a human eye.

The analogy with pens includes some ironic parallels. The word *squid* derives from the Latin word for "reed," and reeds were the source for Roman writing implements. Squid—although writers may not like this thought—have no backbone. In their 400 to 500 million years of evolution, they swapped their original shells for swimming muscles, transforming the vestigial armor into a rigid, penlike structure within the main body. They also carry around a sac of ink, which—and here the analogy with pens and writers surely careens out of control—they squirt to elude predators.

With a few other oddities such as octopi and vampyromorphs, this weird mollusk belongs to the class of *cephalopods,* a term invented from Greek words for "head" and "foot." Some medieval travel narratives contain reports and even pictures of a male figure who sits in the shade provided by a large, umbrellalike foot growing, sole first, directly from his head. The squid comes very close to being a genuine "head-footed" creature. Its head, in fact, contains an exceptionally well-developed brain that gives it the intelligence of some mammals.

Giant squid, found mostly off the coast of Chile, not only have a well-developed brain but also can exceed sixty feet in length and weigh up to one thousand pounds. This intelligent, voracious predator is believed to engage in deadly battles with sperm whales miles beneath the ocean surface. The evidence for these epic struggles consists mostly in the battered remains that float to the surface. Sperm whales, however, are sometimes found with strips of circular scars across the head and jaws—inflicted by the suckers on the giant squid tentacles. The skin looks like a network of moon craters.

The few sailors who have claimed to witness the combat between sperm whales and giant squids report a scene of surreal strangeness. Sharks cruise around the massive combatants. The eyes of the giant squid, according to one witness, were a foot in diameter, eerie and goblinlike, black plates set against the livid whiteness of the head. Ancient tales of sea serpents dragging ships to the bottom may well refer to the carnivorous giant squid. No creature better indicates how vast a gap separates the human-centered world from the mysterious panorama of undersea life. Yet the squid, a perfect emblem for the otherness of nature, can also remind us that humans, too, are a product of the earth and, in fact, not as unique as we often like to think.

For example, squid travel by jet propulsion. They suck water into their body cavity through openings alongside their head and then, using their swimming muscles, expel it at high pressure through a funnel. This mechanism allows them to accelerate rapidly over short distances, like drag racers. At speeds of up to nine feet per second, they can propel their bodies above the surface as if flying. This also makes them formidable predators to marine life both large and small. At night they sometimes come to the surface and feed in numbers so large that they destroy huge quantities of fish stock.

Squid, in turn, are prey to toothed whales, seals, sea lions, tuna, swordfish, sharks and pelagic birds such as petrels and albatrosses. Sperm whales alone are said to eat 100 million tons of squid each year. It's a hard life. Most squid survive less than eighteen months. It takes three hearts to pump enough blood to sustain their powerful bursts of acceleration. Sex occurs only once in a squid's lifetime, and soon afterward it dies. In 1969 the celebrated marine explorer Jacques-Yves Cousteau found his ship *Calypso* completely surrounded by millions of small mating squid. The sea seemed to boil with the thrashing mass. Sharks swam through the thick fields of squid with jaws gaping. Days later, on diving to the bottom in a minisub, Cousteau discovered some 20 million pale cadavers littering the sandy ocean floor.

Squid, however alien their habits, are connected with humans through an ecology that reaches far beyond their place in the food chain. For example, the squid possesses a giant nerve cell almost a millimeter in diameter that has proved immensely valuable for research in cell biology. The synapse of the squid's stellate ganglion—the largest synapse known—gives scientists a fine model for the study of neurotransmission. Research facilities like the famous Marine Biological Laboratory at Woods Hole are full of homely cephalopods busily contributing to the advancement of science.

Yet, beyond Woods Hole and Cousteau's *Calypso*, the main human interest in squid is commercial. The question is simply how to catch them fast enough, hence the value of the immense, thirty-five-mile-long driftnets. When Polish ships a few years ago discovered huge schools of squid in the unregulated South Atlantic waters off Argentina, almost at once ships moved in from Japan, Spain, the Soviet Union, Portugal, South Korea, Taiwan, East Germany and even Bulgaria. Peter Hjul, editor of *Fishing News International,* called it "just about the only free-for-all left in the world." Squid is an excellent source of protein, low in fats and high in essential minerals, and the Asian market seems almost inexhaustible. It is unlikely that the driftnet ships currently operating in the North Pacific will leave this valuable resource to the sharks and sperm whales.

⚓ ⚓ ⚓

The fog rolls in. Now the *Sea Shepherd II* rides ahead half-hidden like a ghost ship. I seem to be losing strength again. A diet consisting entirely of soy milk and granola isn't ideal for two weeks of rough travel, but I don't trust either my stomach or the water supply, and this is no time to abandon my semivegetarian habits of the last ten years. Still, it's hard to concentrate as Paul argues that the time for moderation and compromise is long past.

"It gives me a lot of pride that we haven't won any awards," he says.

Environmental awards, in his view, go to groups that cooperate with the system. But then he amends his statement, remembering a headdress given to him by the Kaipo Indians in Brazil.

Paul wanders off, and I take over the watch for Chris, who badly needs sleep. The fog lifts enough to let me just make out the high stern of the *Sea Shepherd II*. I enter happily into the ritual of watching the ship lumber ahead of us, its thick towrope dropping slack into the water and then pulling tight, over and over in a hypnotic rhythm. There's not much else to do out here but scan the grey haze of the horizon and listen for radio calls.

Suddenly, the towrope snaps! The *Sea Shepherd II* lumbers on ahead, oblivious, while the *Edward Abbey* falls far behind, dead in the water. I rouse Peter from his bunk, who tells me to get the engines started, which means a dash to the engine room. Soon Paul is on the bridge and everyone springs into action.

We haul the long, heavy rope back onboard after ten minutes of hard pulling—at the cost of a long, brass-tipped boat hook that slips out of Scamp's hand and sinks instantly. Paul then revs up the big twin engines and heads toward the now distant *Sea Shepherd II*. As we speed along he notices, about twenty yards off the port side, an oblong, white block the size of a scrub brush. It's a float used to hold up driftnets. A few minutes later a second float bobs past.

Everyone senses that we're closing in.

At 1:15 p.m. I spot a black shape bobbing off the starboard side. Such shapes glide by once or twice a day and turn out to be round black floats from ordinary fishing nets, lost and drifting free. Sometimes the *Sea Shepherd II* will veer off course and try to snag them, with a daredevil like Trevor climbing far out on the pointed steel girder (nicknamed the "can opener") that protrudes from the starboard side. The can opener is designed to prevent opposing ships from coming alongside, but it also makes a good, if risky, perch for snagging floats. The floats are elusive, however, and nobody yet has managed to pull one in.

This time it's not a float. It's a seal! Meg, using binoculars, reports that it has floppy ears like a dog. A fur seal, Paul explains. A good sign, too. The seal apparently wants what the driftnetters want. It is more evidence that we are getting close.

Peter compares our quest to riding a bicycle in search of an eighteen-wheel rig parked somewhere in the Ohio valley. Satellite pictures would let us locate the fleet easily, but, while the U.S. condemns driftnetters, it won't publish the data that would let us find them. The Japanese government, through its fisheries ministry, supports its fleets with the latest satellite technology. We're looking for a needle in a haystack, and

The "can opener," a protruding, sharpened steel girder, protects the side of the *Sea Shepherd II*.

maybe the needle knows we're looking and therefore keeps changing location. At least we may finally be near enough to get lucky.

Paul has been strangely immune to the boredom that has afflicted almost all the crew for the last few days. He must sense that something is about to happen. Besides, he claims that an Earth Warrior is happy anywhere. Boredom just means we're not living fully in the present. But now it's impossible to feel bored or detached or half-present. The fur seal and floats engender a sense that the ocean out here is not as empty as it seemed two hours ago.

⚓ ⚓ ⚓

It's 7:30 p.m. now—North Pacific time. Despite the signs that we're getting close, I'm still tired and weak after days trapped on this floating metal box with little food and no exercise. Before he left Long Beach, Peter strapped a rowing machine to the aft deck. It's a wonderful, crazy image—a rowing machine on a diesel-powered ship—but the seas have been too rough for working out. When I tried a few chin-ups from a structural pipe outside the galley, my body swayed from side to side like a flesh pendulum. My only workout has been simulating bench presses against the metal frame of the upper bunk as I lie on my back below. So far Meg hasn't complained.

My weariness extends to conversation at dinner tonight. Paul launches into a monologue about the Spanish discovery of the Americas, now widely reinterpreted as a Western holocaust carried out against the Native American population. It's hard to imagine the savageness of the Christian response. Columbus and Pizarro fed Indian babies to their dogs. Soldiers held contests to see who could cut an Indian in half with just one swing of the sword. Nazi Germany has nothing on the Spanish conquest of the Americas.

As the talk turns to violence, Paul says he's surprised that the environmental movement (today, too, he's willing to admit that it's a movement, at least for purposes of argument) is so moderate, considering how many people are maimed and killed by the toxic chemicals pumped into our surroundings. The corporations that poison the air and water and food are driven by exactly the same goal that drew Columbus and Pizarro: wealth. What about health? A Russian scientist assigned to provide an official report says that the nuclear disaster and subsequent cleanup at Chernobyl have cost between five thousand and seven thousand lives so far. Over the next fifty years, in the United States alone, the hole in the ozone layer will kill an additional two hundred thousand people from fatal skin cancers. Humans are part of the environment—and as damaged as the rivers.

So the issue of violence is important especially because we need to get straight who constitutes the real threat. Isn't it violence if you pollute and destroy the environment? Businesses now look for good publicity for their belated efforts to protect the environment—efforts often merely cosmetic—but what CEO wants to touch the proposal by World Bank senior economist Herman Daly that the West must shift from a growth-based economy to a stable-state economy? Daly's "stable state" means giving up the dream of endless annual increases in the GNP. It's a self-destructive dream, he argues, because we end up living in a world that has exhausted its natural resources.

Since we continue to erode our health and to destroy the environment in the quest for profit, growth and development—gold, in short—it is clearly a cop-out to condemn environmentalists for acts of violence. Paul readily describes himself as the inventor of tree-spiking, but insists that the tactic has never killed or injured anyone. The aim of spiking trees is to save forests, not injure loggers. This logic requires that spikers always inform logging companies exactly which stands of forest are spiked, and hence too expensive to cut. The only recorded spike injury occurred at a nonunion mill to a worker who was unprotected by the thick Plexiglas shield that nor-

Dressed for action, Paul Watson awaits a run-in with driftnetters.

mally covers the saw. In any case, the spike predated the environmental movement.

Paul puts it this way: The timber companies, looking only for short-term profits in an industry they know is dying, have an incentive to depict environmentalists as murderous tree-spikers while concealing a safety record so bad that the death rate for loggers who do the most dangerous work, at the tree-tops, is over 30 percent.

Tonight, somehow, I can't work up much passion. The talk pushes ahead with a sameness that resembles the miles of grey water surrounding us. Nobody could survive a steady diet of self-righteous environmental doom and gloom. Dying coral reefs off the Florida coast. Acid rain in the Northeast. Toxic dumps in Michigan. Pesticide runoff from Iowa farmland. Oil spills in Alaska. The list drones on. Maybe that's why Paul needs to move from words to action. No matter. Right now I need something—anything—to pick up my spirits.

Paul, by contrast, seems to be gaining energy every hour. He wears his multiple-laced, calf-high World War II ("General Patton") army boots, a black sweater with military-style patches and a long bowie knife secured at his hip by a war-surplus belt. The change of apparel seems significant and communicates an air of menace, unlike his tie-dyed T-shirt and denim shorts. Paul devotes many pages of *Earthforce!* to military tactics. He looks like a man who knows he will have work to do soon, or like someone on a dangerous mission who has sworn that the enemy won't take him alive.

The sunset fills the late evening sky with long, faint streaks of violet and rose, reminding me of the pastel seascapes of German Romantic painter Caspar David Friedrich, with their dark silhouettes of aristocrats in formal dress gazing out at the sea and the hushed dusk sky, as if awaiting a profound revelation. Later, in a different mood, Paul, on the bridge for his usual premidnight watch, reads aloud from Edward Abbey's acerbic book *A Voice Crying in the Wilderness* while the moon casts a misty white glow against the darkness. One of Abbey's aphorisms particularly impresses me tonight: "There has got to be a God. The world could not have become so fucked up by chance alone."

⚓ ⚓ ⚓

At 9:30 P.M. Mark's voice, serious and almost conspiratorial, comes over the radio with an abrupt, enigmatic message: "The kettle is boiling."

"What the *hell* does that mean?" Paul mutters, setting down his book with annoyance.

A long silence follows. Then Mark's voice resumes, sounding a little hurt. "It's the code from the last campaign, remember? We have radar contact at fifteen miles."

The mood on the bridge turns simultaneously tense and manic. As the *Sea Shepherd II* swings sharply in the direction indicated by the radar, Stuart and I laugh like crazy men at the exchange between Mark and Paul. "The kettle is boiling." The homely code gets repeated to everyone who shows up on the bridge, and crew members show up quickly as word spreads that something serious is going on. Mark's spy-novel seriousness and Paul's irritated nonchalance seem to be a perfect and typical Sea Shepherd mismatch. But our laughter contains more than a trace of hysteria. I'm feeling anything but nonchalant as we get closer and closer to the unknown ship.

After ten minutes of anxious waiting, we recognize, outlined against the late evening sky, the shape of a giant cargo vessel piled high with goods most likely on the great circle route from Japan through the Panama Canal. But it's not really a letdown. In 1990 the *Sea Shepherd II* sighted a cargo ship just prior to making contact with the Japanese driftnet fleet. Paul takes note of this omen. Neither the cargo ship nor another like it that appears half an hour later responds to our radio calls. He shakes his head at yet another sign of how times have changed on the high seas.

CHAPTER TEN

ORIGIN OF PROSPERITY

• • •

Twelfth full day at sea. The omens of yesterday evening—the fur seal, driftnet floats and cargo ships—start to look like false prophecy. The hours are long and uneventful as the clouds lower and the sky continues to thicken with grey. The feeling of endlessness grows stronger as the horizon loses its sharp line, blurring and closing in. It gives me the uncanny sense that I am gradually turning invisible, like a traveler in a snowstorm. Meg and I stare out the front windows of the bridge, but although we share the same space it is really a space of two solitudes.

Putting in the last hour of her watch, Meg drifts in and out of focus, half-drowsing. Then she rubs her eyes, rubs them again and radios excitedly to the *Sea Shepherd II*. It is 5:50 P.M.

"You guys see what I see? There's a *ship* off the port bow!" I take a quick breath and feel my stomach drop. An indistinct dark outline shows up against the smoke-grey horizon a few miles ahead. The watch on the *Sea Shepherd II*, caught napping, thinks it's another cargo vessel. Meg is not so sure. It is still only a dark blot in the distance, and the view doesn't get much clearer through our semifunctional binoculars, where I can just make out that the front half of the blot is somewhat lower than the back. Container ships look more like solid blocks. Maybe it's an oil tanker.

Meg darts below to Paul's cabin, and almost at once he bounds up to the bridge. Gazing for a moment through the binoculars, he knows exactly what it is.

"Driftnetter."

His voice conveys something beyond confidence, a blend of elation and eagerness. This is it. This is what he's come for. The long, slow days spent planning, repairing and plodding at eight knots an hour behind the *Sea Shepherd II* disappear as if they never happened. His excitement is catching, and I feel a jolt of elation, but not pure elation. Paul has done this before. He's the expert. I have no experience ramming ships. Hell, I'm barely over my seasickness. Suppose they start shooting?

Paul revs the engines as we cast off the towline that connects us to the *Sea Shepherd II.*

"Hot fuck!" Meg is fired up.

"Where'd she learn to talk like that?" Paul says, amused, to no one in particular. The bridge has quickly filled again with crew members, as the binoculars pass from hand to hand. Meg endures some good-natured teasing, which at least seems to restore shipboard routine. Meanwhile the grey outline on the blurred horizon grows larger and clearer. The banter can't hide the tension we feel. We all know there's no going back.

As we close the distance, I'm wondering if I made the right decision to come along. Is this really where I want to be? It amazes me that everyone on the bridge can't hear my heartbeat.

Paul is surprised we keep gaining so quickly. "I thought they were running from us," he says to Peter. "You'd think they would have heard what we did to them two years ago."

I'm thinking the same thing. Our plans have been no secret, and we're a cinch to track by satellite. It could be a trap.

The ship apparently has just started laying net, and we circle the radar buoy—a large red ball with an antenna—that bobs at the spot where the net begins. After they lay thirty or forty miles of net tonight, Paul explains, the radar buoy will let them circle back in the morning to start pulling it in. We need to proceed cautiously so as not to tangle our propellers in the driftnet. But it's hard. Caution belongs to the slow-motion world we just left behind.

Peter scrambles to start filming and hands me a spare Nikon. It feels heavy, with a motor-driven shutter that makes satisfying, precise, metallic clicks as I test the release button. Peter tells me to shoot the entire roll. Paul grabs the radio mike attached to the ceiling and tries to rouse the *Sea Shepherd II*, which has probably fallen several miles behind us in the thickening fog, out of sight.

"Yo! Homeboy!"

The driftnet captain, if he heard, must be flipping through his phrase book at warp speed. Paul seems to enjoy the idea of ghetto dialect fifteen hundred miles out in the middle of nowhere. "We won't get in trouble, will we?" he asks Peter, pretending to check his radio style for political correctness. As if he cared.

Fortunately, the *Sea Shepherd II* is alert. Paul radios the coordinates of the radar buoy and tells Jon to start pulling in the net. Visibility is down to 150 feet, Jon says, so finding the driftnet may not be easy. Paul and Jon confirm the coordinates for a rendezvous in case they lose radio contact. Then Paul turns up the engines another notch, and the chase is on.

I straddle the open doorway leading from the bridge to the deck. Clamping both hands to the camera, I leave the work of

The Japanese driftnet ship *Gen Ei Maru No. 68* appears!

hanging on mainly to my elbows and knees, which I've jammed against the door frame. Aside from the photographs, my main contribution will be not to fall off. Ken reports that the deck is slick as ice.

In minutes, after pounding through the sea, we are running alongside a large white ship that bears on its bow Asian markings and, just below, as if in translation, the block letters *Gen Ei Maru No. 68*. The ship looms out of the grey mist, a huge chalk cliff with long, soot-black stains disfiguring the port-side hull. Paul says it's a Japanese ship, and I feel immediate relief as my fears of a trap recede. According to Paul, gun laws in Japan make it less likely that Japanese ships will start shooting, so it's unlikely they would draw us into an ambush. Still, he is taking no chances.

"I want everybody to keep down," he says firmly. "Don't make yourself a target."

I've already swapped my new Huskies cap for a beat-up, all-black model that blends with the black paint on the *Edward Abbey*. The crisp white Huskies cap made me feel like a duck in a shooting gallery. Now, however, I simply feel like a black duck in a shooting gallery. Where am I supposed to go? The Japanese crew, in their working blue jumpsuits, glance at us warily as we crouch outside the bridge, watching the pale green monofilament net pour steadily from their stern. With Paul gunning the engines, I turn my cap bill-backwards so it won't blow off and zero in through the Nikon's incredibly clear viewfinder. I smile when I hear the expensive, motor-driven shutter run off a half-dozen shots. Leaning over the waist-high metal barrier outside the bridge that leads down to the deck, I try to focus on the closely spaced, white floats that tumble at high speed from the stern of the *Gen Ei Maru No. 68*. The rapid motion makes it look as if the ship were voiding an immense string of sausagelike excrement. A constant stream of water shoots across the net as it plays out, keeping the floats from tangling with the lead weights that will hold the extended net perpendicular.

Word comes back from the *Sea Shepherd II* that they've located the radar buoy and started retrieval operations. Paul, calm but pleased, is savoring victory.

"We got ourselves a net!"

But the victory is incomplete or at least premature. Shortly after Jon begins to haul in the net, we hear that the *Sea Shepherd II* has stopped retrieval operations while it sends a zodiac to inspect the propellers, as they suspect the props are matted with driftnet. Paul warns Jon to be careful.

"Those nets are dangerous to dive on."

On their last trip a professional diver panicked when he got tangled in driftnet, and only a quick-thinking rescue by Peter got him out alive.

"I want everybody to keep down," Paul repeats. "I don't want too high a profile until we determine what their reaction is."

We pull closer to the stern with its elevated platform and high-speed drum where the sausage factory spews out its net. "Check out those guys on the back," Paul orders. "Have they got any guns or anything?"

We don't see any weapons as we edge closer. A few of the Japanese crew members even pause to smile and wave. They probably haven't seen another ship for weeks, and common courtesy makes me feel momentarily like waving back. But I resist the temptation. These are not fishermen, I remind myself, but industrial workers employed by corporations a thousand miles away concerned only with sucking every last drop of profit out of the sea. Normal courtesies do not apply. Later I learn that the old-style Kanji script on the bow of the *Gen Ei Maru No. 68* translates as "Origin of Prosperity." The ironies are too obvious.

Soon the smiles stop, to be replaced by hostile glares and lewd hip-thrusting gestures as the *Edward Abbey* dogs the *Gen Ei Maru No. 68* at top speed. We're now racing close together, side by side. Paul orders Scamp to cover up the cannon on our stern in preparation to pass the Japanese ship.

As we cut periodically in front of their bow, I wince like a kid on a roller coaster, but I love it, too. It's the kind of elation that comes with taking chances and breaking rules, sheer animal energy cut loose. At the same time, I concentrate on keeping my grip as the *Edward Abbey* slams against the waves. The noise of our twin diesel engines has risen to a wild roar. As I duck back onto the bridge, I hear the jumbo windshield wipers slapping away like a racing pulse. Spray covers everything.

Peter climbs outside and, using a harness, straps himself to the small tower atop the bridge—a towel tucked inside the harness to wipe off his lens. This is what he lives for. Paul zigzags for dramatic shots, racing the engines to put us half a mile in front of the Japanese ship and then turning us sharply 180 degrees to approach head-on, in a full-speed collision course. As the gap closes, my euphoria takes a dive and I press my knees against the door frame even tighter, calculating the quickest route to jump overboard.

Jumping overboard, even to avoid a collision, is not such a great idea. On my first night aboard the *Sea Shepherd II,* I helped transfer a large pile of heavy orange bags to the *Edward Abbey.* Stamped in black on each bag were the words "Immersion Suit." What's an immersion suit? Later Peter explained that a person wouldn't last twenty minutes in the freezing North Pacific without these watertight, insulated jumpsuits. A life jacket just gives you twenty minutes to freeze to death. The sharks would do you a favor if they got you first.

Nobody ever bothered to show us how to put on an immersion suit. Would there be time to learn? Paul veers aside at the last moment, so I thankfully postpone my acquaintance with the big orange bags.

Peter climbs back inside the bridge, drenched and cradling his camera with its super-sixteen-millimeter lens, eyes bright with pleasure. We ask him if he got the head-on shot. "That's why I get the big bucks," he replies. I hand him the Nikon. The chase, meanwhile, looks like it won't end soon, and Paul sends for a bowl of food so he won't have to leave the bridge. Corn chowder is Stuart's single menu item tonight. Even though the dinner hour has long passed, I can't eat—but I need to do *something* besides cling to the open doorway of the bridge, so I figure I'll get my camera and take some more photos.

I stumble below deck, grabbing with every step at whatever handhold I can find—tabletop, metal stair, bulkhead—as we bounce and churn at top speed. On the way, I pass the open door of Paul's cabin, which he must have left ajar hours ago in his haste to reach the bridge. My stomach drops as I see what is neatly laid out on his bed: two well-oiled semiautomatic rifles.

⚓ ⚓ ⚓

We continue to chase the Japanese ship at speeds around fourteen knots. With night falling, the *Sea Shepherd II* now lags about thirty miles behind us in the fog and deepening blackness. For a short time we lose radio contact almost completely. We can hear them but they can't hear us. Again my confidence drops as yet another crucial instrument fails.

By 9:15 P.M. the *Gen Ei Maru No. 68* has stopped. Then it starts up again. The bright flood lamps surrounding the work area show that something unusual is going on. Normally a driftnet ship waits five or six hours, while the crew sleeps, before circling back to the radar buoy where it will pull in the net. Paul radios Jon that the Japanese ship seems to be pulling in the net right now, without waiting or circling back, which suggests an impending confrontation. While the Japanese are pulling in the driftnet at one end, the *Sea Shepherd II* is pulling it in at the other. Sometime tonight the two ships are bound to meet.

"That'll be amusing," Paul chuckles.

I fail to see the humor.

But soon we have our own problems to deal with. As the *Gen Ei Maru No. 68* goes its way pulling in driftnet, we prepare to inspect our propellers, which are acting sluggish. I get a sick feeling as I watch the floating nylon filament billow underneath the hull of the *Edward Abbey*, almost a sure sign that driftnet is wrapped around the propellers. Grabbing a flashlight, Paul sets the engine on idle and heads back to inspect the stern.

Immediately we begin to rock wildly as the idled engines leave us at the whim of the sea. Scamp, meanwhile, races down to his bunk and changes into shorts. Moments later there's an unmistakable splash as he dives overboard to cut us free. The lights of the *Gen Ei Maru No. 68* recede and we rock helplessly in the darkness. At last Scamp, hair plastered down to his nose, pads barefoot and soaking wet toward the bridge—flashing a big grin.

He's cut us free! Paul slowly increases our speed and the crisis passes.

Not for long, however. As we start back toward the distant Japanese ship, Paul shines his spotlight over the starboard side to search for the elusive driftnet. Within minutes he spots the telltale white Styrofoam floats that lie between us and the *Gen Ei Maru No. 68.* Scamp thinks we can ride over the net if we gun the engines to top speed and then cut the props. The experiment fails, however, and again we are tangled. Once more, Scamp races past for his shorts. I go to my cabin to add a sweatshirt beneath my windbreaker. It's getting very cold as well as very dark. In the black middle distance I can see a strobe beacon attached to the driftnet, pulsing its methodical beam.

The weather must be getting worse because the *Edward Abbey* now rocks violently with our engines on idle. Standing watch on the bridge, I hear a loud and substantial crash in the radio room. Now what? Somehow Peter's massive super-sixteen camera has come free from its crevice and fallen all the way down to the crew's quarters. It lies at the bottom of the steep ladder like a corpse.

Steadied against the violent motion of the ship, I quickly summon Peter, who groans as he struggles with the misshapen camera to learn how bad the damage is. He holds up a piece of broken glass and tries to find where it fits, without success.

"A ten thousand–dollar fall," he moans quietly. "Ten thousand dollars."

At 11:15 p.m. Scamp finally emerges from the freezing water and we break free from the driftnet. Or temporarily free. I stand half-outside the bridge to shuttle messages between Paul and the crew as we head full-speed back toward the almost indistinguishable lights of the *Gen Ei Maru No. 68*. We pause and detour continually to avoid the driftnet—and each time we lose our bearings as the Japanese ship recedes still farther. Paul can't leave the wheel and the bridge restricts his vision, so I stand outside as an extra pair of eyes, searching the blackness for signs. What I see makes almost no sense.

With some apprehension I report to Paul that there seems to be more than one set of lights. The bright yellow glow looks too near for the *Sea Shepherd II*, which should still be many miles to the east. So a third ship must know we are out here, slicing precariously through this web of driftnet. Paul turns our course east to rendezvous with the *Sea Shepherd II*, but it soon becomes apparent that all of us—the *Edward Abbey*, the *Gen Ei Maru No. 68*, and the unknown third ship—are headed in the same direction. I ask Paul if he has any idea what will happen when the *Gen Ei Maru No. 68* meets the *Sea Shepherd II*.

He laughs. "No."

Dark clouds streak the midnight horizon. The *Sea Shepherd II* appears as a bright light off the port side. As we contact Sue by radio, her voice sounds deliberately measured, which makes it clear they are in trouble. Because of the open channel, she keeps the details vague. We are meanwhile rocking and bucking at top speed through heavy seas. The constant threat of running over driftnet means we need a lookout posted near the apex of the plunging bow. So Meg and Stuart stand there at the edge of Paul's spotlight, outlined against the dark sky and wild sea, wedged in their yellow-orange rain gear against the low guard-wire that barely keeps them from pitching headlong into the waves. One slip on the lurching, slippery deck and they'll be swept under the ship and killed instantly.

We shout messages back and forth. They frighten me, Meg and Stuart, ordinary people, disturbed at the ruin of the environment, doing whatever is needed in circumstances that would ordinarily freeze the bones with dread.

⚓ ⚓ ⚓

The confusion and incompetence are getting me down. Peter has been repairing his camera with chess-master concentration, blocking out everything else in the universe. ("About sixteen different broken pieces.") Like the crew of the *Sea Shepherd II*, we spend most of the night trying to untangle our props from the miles of floating driftnet ropes undulating just below the surface.

Paul explodes. "It's a goddamn spiderweb!"

We've certainly lost the advantage of surprise. The captain of the *Gen Ei Maru No. 68* must be on the phone to Tokyo right now. The Japanese ministry of fisheries often keeps patrol boats in the area, supposedly to check on violations, but mostly to help the driftnet fleet locate squid. They've had plenty of time to plan a response. All this delay is unnerving. And what's going on with that third set of lights? Peter thinks it's another driftnet ship.

The *Edward Abbey*, when it left Long Beach, had just been equipped with a special propeller guard to prevent entanglement with driftnet, but clearly the guard didn't work, so Scamp has been diving into water so black and bitterly cold that it must be like diving into pain. The propeller guard got bent on a floating log on the way to Santa Cruz, Paul figures. As an economy move, Peter had decided against buying underwater lights, so Scamp must dive for the propellers and cut us free mostly by feel. He seems to be our regular answer to failure, ineptitude and emergency, but surely he has limits. A testy, professorial voice in my head asks what is wrong with a little foresight.

It's well after midnight—12:40 A.M.—when we at last reach the *Sea Shepherd II*. I feel immensely reassured by its sturdy bulk, like meeting an old friend, and our two ships idling about fifty yards apart generate a warm pool of light against the starless black sky. But the reassurance doesn't last. Jon figures they confiscated about a half-mile of driftnet before the propellers tangled. The *Sea Shepherd II*, however, with its much larger and deeper propellers, is tangled so severely that Jon needs to send down a diver with air tanks. All their air tanks are empty, so the *Sea Shepherd II* is completely immobilized until we supply replacements.

Why don't they have full air tanks? Don't ask. We're rocking so badly with our engines cut that it's almost suicidal to try to launch a half-ton zodiac from our aft deck, but there's no other way to transfer an air tank to the *Sea Shepherd II*. The zodiac swings crazily overhead on the winch, transforming its 115-horsepower outboard motor into a lethal weapon. But somehow we get it in the water. Half an hour after launching the zodiac, still nothing has happened. Why not? The air tank we sent over is empty. Why did we send an empty tank? Don't ask.

The empty tank comes back for refilling, which requires more treacherous work on the slick, tipping deck. Then it takes two additional trips to get Randy, the diver, outfitted with a proper wet suit. Watching the vegan crew of the *Sea Shepherd II* stand on deck eating from their omnipresent bowls, even Paul gets testy. "Vegans are always eating," he seethes. "That's why we can't get any net." Anxious and frustrated, I scan the horizon for the lights of Japanese patrol boats.

It takes until 1:15 A.M. to get Randy equipped. Peter joins one of the zodiac trips to retrieve his backup camera. He says he doesn't feel so bad about the broken one, but then I suspect it would take thermonuclear war to damage Peter's optimism. There are lights on the horizon now and they seem to be getting closer. Scamp suddenly appears on the bridge and shouts that we need to get some oil in the port engine "real quick," then disappears.

Sitting at the radiophone under a macabre green bulb, I try to write, thinking that almost anything could happen next. At about 2:00 A.M., with no crisis imminent, I figure I'd better get a few minutes rest. I crawl into my sleeping bag, not bothering to remove my shoes, cap or windbreaker.

I can't sleep, of course, but the bunk provides shelter from the slow-motion chaos on deck. Yet I must have dozed off, because suddenly Meg is yelling that I'd better come up on deck fast. She sounds deadly serious, so I'm on my feet immediately, climbing the metal ladder toward the bridge. The scene looks nothing like the well-lit midnight rendezvous. It's 5:30 A.M. In the predawn greyness I can make out the powerful black shape of the *Sea Shepherd II* swinging behind us in a wide arc. Directly ahead, close enough to hit with a heavy stone, is the white stern of the big driftnet ship *Gen Ei Maru No. 79*.

Number 79? What happened to Number 68? But there's no time to find out. The superstructure of the two ships, strung with wires and lights, looks like a midocean Christmas scene. The Japanese ship rocks softly in the early morning gloom, large and bulky enough to absorb the waves, while the *Edward Abbey* still rolls and lurches just a few yards behind. Meanwhile the *Sea Shepherd II* rounds its arc and now pulls almost parallel with us about a quarter-mile away. What's happening? Paul is nowhere in sight.

"Paul transferred to the *Sea Shepherd,*" Peter says.

So the question of where I will stay during the action has been decided by fate. I don't know if I'm relieved. I'm mostly bewildered, aware that there's nothing I can do but hold on—hold on and hope that the errors, difficulties and confusions don't culminate in one gigantic terrible mistake.

Peter, as first mate, has charge of the *Edward Abbey*, but he's mostly concerned about getting good pictures when the *Sea Shepherd II* rams into the *Gen Ei Maru No. 79*, so he installs Scamp at the bridge. He likes the way Scamp steers us in extra close. Scamp's total recklessness must remind Peter of his own early days spent hanging out of planes filming skiers, skydivers and stuntmen. He knows you don't get great film by playing it safe.

Scamp brings us in even closer behind the *Gen Ei Maru No. 79*, while off our port side the *Sea Shepherd II* picks up speed. Then—flat out, horn blaring—Paul steers his big black ship right toward the middle of the *Gen Ei Maru No. 79*.

I don't quite believe what I'm seeing: three ships in the predawn mist huddled together like a small outpost of civilization in all this emptiness; then the big black ship insanely drives toward the Japanese vessel at full speed as if to cut it in half.

I brace my legs against the protective flange outside the bridge of the *Edward Abbey* and see blue-suited Japanese workers scrambling for safety. The Japanese captain must not know what's happening, or maybe he can't increase his speed fast enough to get away. The collision looks inescapable. Scamp revs up our engines to a near-scream, and all I can do is focus my camera and swallow hard. Swallowing takes almost an act of will.

The *Sea Shepherd II* presses on inexorably toward the Japanese ship. Paul is aiming to hit the stern with its all-important net-retrieval machinery. The *Sea Shepherd II* rushes across the last fifty yards of open water. I'm feeling trapped in a dream spinning out of control as I watch the lumbering black ship plunge ahead, now just a few feet away from the stern of the *Gen Ei Maru No. 79*. Two mastodons or dinosaurs crashing together in combat might seem less terrifying and prodigious. The shuddering crunch of metal on metal is seconds away, but all I can hear is our screaming engines and the loud blaring horn on the *Sea Shepherd II*.

The two huge steel beasts converge.

From our position I can't see exactly what is happening. It's clear that the *Sea Shepherd II* has ripped the net completely off the drum. Maybe, in a reptilian layer of my brain fascinated by disaster, I'm just a little disappointed that the Japanese ship is still intact, but the chilling spectacle has left me with no desire to see more. This is an open assault at sea, ship against ship, and the attack is still continuing. Later I learn that Paul veered aside at the last second, missing the Japanese vessel by inches. One Japanese workman inexplicably had remained on the stern, and a direct hit would have killed him, so Paul swerved—but prepared at once for a second strike.

There's no time for a detailed appraisal or even a clear thought, however, as the Japanese captain—suddenly freed from the drag of his net—now opens up the full power of his engines.

The *Gen Ei Maru No. 79* is already taking off at top speed as Paul swings the *Sea Shepherd II* into position for a second strike. Scamp

Sea Shepherd II makes a run at the *Gen Ei Maru No. 79.*

guns our engines still higher and holds the *Edward Abbey* in close pursuit. The stench as we again draw near the Japanese ship is nauseating. "The smell of death" is how Paul describes the odor of these driftnet factories, but it's not dead fish or even diesel fuel I smell now. The *Sea Shepherd II* crew has scored a direct hit with vials of butyric acid, and it's the butyric acid lobbed onto its deck that makes the Japanese ship reek like a thousand pounds of rancid butter. I duck inside the bridge to avoid vomiting. Nobody could work long in those fumes, which is the purpose behind the butyric acid vials. The *Gen Ei Maru No. 79* will set no more driftnet on this voyage.

A half-familiar noise startles me as we punch through the deepening swells. Something isn't right. Is it gunfire? Before I can grasp what's happening we get an urgent message. Paul has been pushing the *Sea Shepherd II* to top speed and now the water pump has broken down. Once again I'm not surprised. As overheated engines could burn up and leave us stranded in the middle of the North Pacific, Paul has no choice but to stop the *Sea Shepherd II*—one more time—for repairs.

His voice over the radio is unemotional and businesslike, as usual, but the disgust is easy to imagine. He had told Jon to have a backup system ready. Now the *Sea Shepherd II* is out of action indefinitely.

"We're dead in the water," Paul comments dryly over the radio.

But it's not over. Paul orders Peter to continue the chase in the *Edward Abbey*. More specific instructions follow. As Scamp pulls us close to the racing driftnet ship, Peter runs below deck and returns holding an AK-47 semiautomatic rifle. Ah yes! So much for denial. Peter shouts directions to Scamp and disappears out the door of the bridge. Shots from the armor-piercing rifle blast through the engine noise. Jesus! The rifle fire almost stops my heartbeat, and I instinctively take cover. Peter is apparently shooting at the bow, aiming below the waterline, where it's mostly storage space. But who knows for sure? *Blam!* Then a deeper, fuller, heart-ripping *boom!* The Civil War cannon on our stern has just fired off a round.

My ears hurt, the smell of gunpowder fills my nose and all is sheer chaos. This is not just more than I bargained for. It's like waking up on a battlefield.

At a loss for what to do, I look around for a safe place to keep taking notes. I feel less vulnerable if I'm writing—a task helps blot out fear—or maybe writing for me still retains a trace of voodoo. I remember reading about an ancient stone slab covered with hieroglyphic script that Egyptian priests ritually doused with water, so that the water would pick up magic power from the writing. I could use some magic now. I remember, too, Peter's warning that the thin metal sides of the *Edward Abbey* are like tin against a high-impact bullet.

"Just so you know," he added. "I'd hit the deck flat on my stomach."

My mouth is now *very* dry.

We radio the Japanese captain to stop, but he clearly has no intention of doing so. I wouldn't stop. Not after someone in a menacing black ship with a black pirate flag has tried to ram my ship in the middle of nowhere. Paul orders Peter to fire across the bow. Shots blast out again. Peter is now holding a shotgun. Where did *that* come from? Then back to the AK-47. He flatly refuses an order to shoot out the spotlight on the *Gen Ei Maru No. 79.*

"It's too close to the bridge," he protests. "A shot would go right *through* the bridge."

Amid the noise and jumble of events I sit at the radiophone hutch and take notes, climb the few stairs to the bridge, return to the hutch, climb to the bridge. It's hard to tell if the Japanese ship is shooting back or just trying to outrun us. Sometimes both ships drop their speed, running neck and neck, before cranking up again. The scream of engines is almost deafening, and my jeans get soaked when I kneel on deck to keep from slipping. Why are we chasing them? They won't stop, we can't capture them and we're not big enough to ram them. Maybe Paul hopes we'll force them to break down.

On a run past the bridge, Chris offers a different theory: "We're just trying to give them the creeps."

Heading below deck, I pass Meg, who is slumped on the bottom rung of the stairs outside our cabin. It's where I found Peter's smashed camera last night, which now seems like years ago. The confusion on deck must be getting to both of us because we have both sought out the point—deep down amidships—where an armor-piercing bullet would do the least damage. She holds her head like someone suffering from a migraine. "This is too radical for me," Meg says.

I'm inclined to agree. I'd like to be sympathetic, and in my crash-calm state I try to say something consoling, but it doesn't work. I'm in no position to offer consolation. Everything that resembles normal life has suddenly blown up in my face. I'm just trying to bluff my way through, trying not to fall apart, hoping that Paul has gotten enough hits and Peter enough pictures. But I doubt it. This is why they've come.

CHAPTER ELEVEN

CONAN AND THE *NAGUAL*

• • •

The sky is grey and the sea is grey. Color seems to have drained from the universe. It's the kind of day when everything goes wrong.

"I'm getting too old for this stuff."

Paul's tired smile is meant to contradict his words. The words, however, linger in the air, canceled but not erased by the smile. Our main business—after the *Gen Ei Maru No. 79* has disappeared in the direction of Tokyo at top speed—is simply to retrieve as much driftnet as possible using the industrial-strength winch installed on the side of the *Sea Shepherd II*. But new obstacles arise almost every hour.

The only bright spot is the square of feltlike red fabric that Paul—after a quick ice-cold shower—drapes over his wet hair, corsair-style, as he sits on the bridge of the *Edward Abbey* eating a bowl of pasta. The fabric might be just a makeshift towel, but it looks like exotic, ceremonial battle gear. Despite the pasta and casual pose, Paul is scanning the horizon for possible intruders. His mood soon turns dark as the net-retrieval operation aboard the *Sea Shepherd II* slows to a stop.

Why the slow pace? The animal-rights vegan crew pauses every few minutes to liberate the squid dangling from the net. Sue carefully cuts the net around each trapped squid to prevent further damage. Hands cupped, other crew members then carry the squid—many just mangled corpses—to port side and slip them gently into the sea. "Go, little squid. Be free"—so runs the carnivorous *Edward Abbey* parody. Never have the contrasting styles of the two ships come so clearly into conflict. Paul radios Jon that he wants the net fast and doesn't give a damn what happens to the squid.

The conflict extends beyond net retrieval to almost every possible procedure. The young *Sea Shepherd II* crew works mostly by consensus, so they consume endless time in discussion, which drives Peter crazy. "I'm a do-it sort of guy," he insists. "I say, don't talk about it, just do it." He knows, too, that Paul is nearing the point of explosion. Peter climbs into the zodiac and shuttles across to "splain" things to the crew. His explanations can be very direct, no concern for hard feelings, and not everyone aboard the *Sea Shepherd II* is fond of Peter right now. This time his threats and "just do it" lecture prove useless. The net merely dribbles in.

The independence of the *Sea Shepherd II* crew infuriates Paul almost as much as their slow pace. He has no room for democratic processes aboard ship. He likes to quote Captain Kirk from *Star Trek,* who once cut down a crew member with the acerbic comment "When this ship is run as a democracy, you'll be the first to know."

It's a standoff. Paul doesn't care about the squid, and the *Sea Shepherd II* crew doesn't care about his orders. The diffuse structure of authority that Paul favors on land works against him out here. He seems to relish his account of discipline in the heyday of the British navy: a captain would tie an offending sailor to the prow and leave him suspended above the waves with a knife, a loaf of bread and three choices. You died of starvation, you cut the rope and drowned or you stabbed yourself. Discipline was no problem back then.

The problem now, however, threatens to escalate into an ugly conflict. Who's in charge here? Jon's long-winded explanation about why he can't force the crew to follow Paul's orders just exasperates Paul further. Moreover, Paul had recently appointed Myra and Sue to the Sea Shepherd board of directors, so their opposition rankles like a betrayal. The frustrations reduce him to threatening to retire the *Sea Shepherd II*, but it's pretty much a hollow threat. Everybody knows Paul has talked about scuttling the ship on this campaign. His attempts at intimidation aren't any more effective than Peter's, which only makes him angrier.

Then there are the technical difficulties. Because the *Sea Shepherd II* works so slowly, the slack driftnet keeps billowing toward the stern and snagging the propellers. It was a bad idea to put the winch amidships. Paul's best effort to speed things up consists finally in putting Scamp and Sam aboard a zodiac to cut free the tangled propellers, but not even Scamp can fix everything. Soon the zodiac and the *Sea Shepherd II* are both snagged in the tough, crisscrossed ropes and monofilament netting. The circus is turning dangerous.

The danger only increases after Scamp finally cuts the zodiac loose. Chris stands on deck watching fretfully as he pilots the zodiac at top speed between the two ships, like a kid in a sportscar, while the grey mist spreads and the waves toss higher. The weather is getting worse by the minute. At the bow of the *Edward Abbey*, Chris seems suddenly almost fearful as she watches Scamp. I wonder if I was mistaken in thinking she is invulnerable. Others, too, notice the difference.

"Hey, it's a chick thing," she shouts aggressively. "It's a chick thing. I worry about him. Okay?"

The delay and confusion at least take a turn toward comedy when Paul sends Stuart, clad in his cook's apron, over to the *Sea Shepherd II* to requisition a few squid for dinner. As Stuart climbs off the zodiac and starts toward the net, Sue extends her knife menacingly. She's deadly serious. Touch this squid, cook, and you die. Stuart backs off immediately, wide-eyed. Sue will let no one—not even Paul—benefit from what she regards as crimes against nature. In this case she backs up her philosophy with a nine-inch blade.

The *Sea Shepherd II* gathers in driftnet.

Today the chief beneficiaries of her philosophy turn out to be the albatrosses. Dozens of the big brown seabirds ride the waves along the invisible, sinuous trajectory of the driftnet, as if perched at a lunch counter. The lunch could be fatal. At least one dead albatross has turned up among the squid, salmon and tuna dangling in the net already pulled in. The difficult question may be who or what *isn't* threatened by the driftnet? I'm beginning to appreciate what it means to hang an immense, invisible, nylon meshwork of two-inch squares that stretches some thirty-five miles. Imagine fleets of one hundred ships all setting their thirty-five miles of net each night. It's not fishing. There's been nothing like it in the history of the planet.

I'm feeling squidlike, trapped, frustrated by the apparently endless delays. I don't like hanging around the scene of the crime, in weather that just keeps getting worse. Our ships have never looked so small and vulnerable, two weeks from land, aimlessly rocking, lurching and circling. It's getting hard to locate the net in the thick, grey, choppy haze of sky and water. Let's get the hell out of here. My heart momentarily surges when Peter recommends to Paul that we just sink the remaining net with a few well-placed buckets of cement.

"A tedious business," Paul mutters at 3:30 in the afternoon, with the sky cold, damp and lowering, visibility almost zero, our spirits dropping in this hostile sea.

⚓ ⚓ ⚓

We're heading home!

Paul makes the decision late in the afternoon with the mist and fog so dense it's impossible to spot the white driftnet floats. With no floats visible, we have no idea where the net is, so we can't sink it or avoid it. Who knows where it will have drifted by tomorrow? Each aimless circle simply increases the chances that we'll end up tangled again, and the sea is so wild now that Scamp wouldn't stand a chance of cutting us free. Our effort to winch the heavy, swinging zodiac back onto the aft deck of the *Edward Abbey* comes one inch from driving the massive, bladed outboard motor into Stuart's skull. I recall Paul's statement that he saw a sailor decapitated by a metal guy-wire that suddenly snapped.

Every hour of delay makes it much more likely that the Japanese will find us.

The driftnet industry claims that lost or abandoned net soon balls up and sinks. Maybe so. There must be hundreds of miles of so-called ghost net out here, killing everything in its path before it finally sinks in a compacted mass of nylon, floats, rope and rotting carcasses. Everyone feels bad about the ghost net we've left behind, but despite all the problems, the *Sea Shepherd II* has also managed to drag onboard several miles of captured driftnet. Stored in the hold, the net makes a pile so thick and spongy that crew members on deck jump down onto it, like kids leaping off the roof of a playhouse.

Our change of course, due east, takes me by surprise. Alaska lies a thousand miles to the north, Hawaii a thousand miles to the south, but Paul picks a fifteen-hundred-mile route to Vancouver Island on the west coast of British Columbia. He's not thinking about which course makes us harder to track. Anyone who wants us badly enough can track us by satellite, and we're too slow to escape. He's thinking that our assault on two Japanese ships in international waters may well stir up political trouble. Paul knows a few Canadian government ministers and thinks he stands a far better chance in Canada than with the antienvironmental Bush administration. I hope he's right.

Everyone is exhausted after thirty-six hours with almost no rest. But not too tired to celebrate. When Sue and Myra weren't looking, Stuart managed to slip a couple of squid and a large tuna into his brown shopping bag, and ever since he's been putting together a seafood feast. He improvises without a recipe, a true kitchen artist. Flattened into milky steaks half an inch thick and flavored with lemon, the fresh squid tastes as good as lobster or salmon. The tuna, just a few hours out of the water, is unbelievably mild and flavorful. French real estate agents (the world masters of overdescription) would be hard-pressed to invent adequate praise.

Dinner finds everyone laughing and telling stories, with Stuart and Meg prominent. Perhaps sheer adrenaline propels them. But they are also veterans now, tested, and they've come through like champions. The jokes imply that they belong. Their elated new sense of belonging hits me sharply, even painfully, because I can't join in with a whole heart. The shots fired and the lost driftnet bother me. This isn't what I thought it would be. And finally, though I tried to help during the encounter with the Japanese, I wasn't truly a crew member with the same duties and the same risks, like Meg and Stuart hanging on in the wild darkness watching for driftnet as we plunged ahead. Besides, writing can easily turn you into an outsider.

The dinnertime stories—most told with a comic twist—focus on the last thirty-six hours. Stuart retells the tale of his heroic, knife-point theft of the squid. Other tales recount the history of the two *Sea Shepherd*s, with their weird cast of characters. For Stuart's enlightenment Paul talks about the Hari Krishna cook who, given a bountiful catch to prepare for dinner, served up a broth composed entirely of fish heads and fish tails, throwing away the rest. My favorite story concerns Dolphin Dave, who has somehow helped ease my feelings of isolation. Dave actually believed he was a dolphin, and Paul finally threw him off the ship in Key West. When Dave demanded to know why, Paul said it was because Dave was crazy.

"Prove it!" challenged Dave.

"Well," said Paul, "for one thing, you're not a dolphin."

"Prove it!" Dave snapped back.

I guess Paul figured he shouldn't have to prove to a dolphin that it wasn't a dolphin, so Dave went. When the *Sea Shepherd II* finally completed the long trip, via the Panama Canal, from Key West to Long Beach, who was waiting there to meet them at the dock? You guessed it.

⚓ ⚓ ⚓

It takes another dangerous and tricky operation to reattach the towline linking the *Edward Abbey* to the *Sea Shepherd II*. Once it's done, however, the long trip back to land promises sizable time for talking and relaxing, free from the anxieties of an imminent ship-ramming engagement. The *Edward Abbey* has an informal circulating library, limited to four issues of *Playboy*, three issues of the comic book *Conan the Barbarian* and an illustrated paperback copy of Coleridge's *Rime of the Ancient Mariner*.

So far I've resisted *Playboy*, for reasons of mental health. I've also resisted Coleridge, because his poem describes a disaster at sea in which almost everyone dies. The voyage turns deadly after the mariner shoots an albatross.

Watching our faithful companion fly alongside the ship for days, I now understand why sailors would consider it bad luck—or even a terrible crime—to kill an albatross. (They also would fish for albatross with baited hooks when meat got scarce.) Shooting the albatross is more than a metaphor for our disharmony with the natural world. It expresses an arrogance and even a submerged hatred that extends to whatever we cannot conquer or tame or turn to profit. Environmentalists would find the moral of the poem a good one: "He prayeth well, who loveth well / Both man and bird and beast."

So that leaves me with *Conan.* Meanwhile Scamp, in a satirical mood, requests a transfer to the *Sea Shepherd II* because, he complains, the *Edward Abbey* is full of senior citizens. I tell him over an issue of *Conan* that for me, just waking up each morning is a near-death experience, and he nods as if nothing were more likely.

⚓ ⚓ ⚓

Coleridge's albatross provides one image of the supernatural or spiritual forces within nature. Paul, too, regards the earth as sacred. For him, a redwood forest evokes the same reverence that Jews attribute to the Wailing Wall or that Muslims attribute to the holy city of Mecca or that Catholics attribute to St. Peter's in Rome. Paul, in his own way, is deeply spiritual, but he finds his source of spiritual awe in nature. Of course the Bible says that God expects us to be good stewards of the natural world, and most religious traditions make a show of revering their deity's handiwork. But stewardship is an anthropocentric office, and most people *act* as if God, or their supreme deity, had assigned human beings the far loftier role of property owners. We pump out the oil and cut down the trees and dig out the minerals. Leaving what to steward or revere? A pumped-out, dug-out, toxic shell?

Most religious traditions place an enlightened or semidivine human figure at the center of their belief. This has opened up a gulf between human beings—whose souls make them nominees for salvation or enlightenment—and the rest of nature, often depicted as fallen, corrupt or merely material. Animals cluster around Satan. The wilderness is filled with monsters descended from Cain. A recoil from the earth is so common that many cultures locate sacredness outside the natural world: above or beyond the earth. Heaven. Olympus. Valhalla. Paul, by contrast, sees the entire planet and all its life forms as a source of sacred feeling.

"Life is more complicated than we can ever hope to imagine," he writes in *Earthforce!* "The diversity of life is infinite relative to the finite ability of the human mind to comprehend."

For Paul, the boundless, the immeasurable, the numinous and the sacred, in other words, are not relocated to an unearthly realm or encrypted in a few grandiose symbols of otherworldliness, like sea and mountains. They are all around us. His biocentrism thus contains something of a mystical streak, and he acknowledges sources of power in the cosmos that people schooled on Western rationalism often dismiss as nonsense. On the bridge he's been reading again from Castaneda's *Tales of Power*. Poor Castaneda keeps trying to maintain his balance by seeking rational explanations for the strange and illogical events to which his Yaqui teacher, Don Juan, introduces him, like walking through a brick wall or jumping up to the top of a high cliff. A warrior, Don Juan patiently instructs him, opens himself to the influx of power that flows mostly unseen and unknown within the familiar world. His term for this suprarational power (so unnerving it can leave Castaneda shattered and near death) is the *nagual*.

"The *nagual*," Don Juan says, to Castaneda's perplexity and discomfort, "is the part of us for which there is no description—no words, no names, no feelings, no knowledge." Paul must have something like the *nagual* in mind when he writes that the Earth Warrior serves the biosphere.

The sacredness of the earth, of course, does not mean that it is untouchable. The question is *how* to touch it. With reverence? Or with ignorance, contempt and greed? Probably one reason why contradictions don't seem to bother Paul is that—like the *nagual* and the idea of the sacred—they expose the limits of rationalism. Rationalists are always trying to catch him in self-contradictions, as if anyone convicted of a flaw in logic is automatically contemptible. For example, how can he believe in the sacredness of the earth and still live in L.A., drive a car, eat meat, drink rum and otherwise coexist with the world he opposes?

This question suggests a belief or wish that environmentalists like Paul can be exposed, at bottom, as pretenders, frauds or hypocrites. They can't really live the pure lives they recommend. It's as if his opponents expect Paul to validate his credentials, so to speak, through daily rites of asceticism, self-denial and saintlike renunciation of the world. But he makes no pretense to philosophical or theological purity. Why renounce the world if the earth is the source of sacredness? Puritanism of any kind offends his appetite for life. When pressed to account for his running satire on vegans, Paul points to their ritualized, quasireligious belief system, complete with the modern equivalents of hair shirts and self-flagellation.

"The fault I find in veganism," he says, "and I've known an awful lot of them, is that they're looking for something which sets them apart as superior, which to me is contradictory to the warrior's way of looking at yourself as a part of the world, not superior or inferior. You can't go and say to the rest of the people, 'I am superior.'"

If the entire biosphere is sacred, are beans less or more sacred than pigs? Cows—Paul calls them artificial animals—are not an endangered species. If the entire public suddenly stopped eating meat, he argues, we might simply escalate an already intolerable pressure on the oceans. Demands for purity and noncontradiction, then, constitute a trap engineered by people uncomfortable with their own compromised lives, who would prefer to see warriors like Paul self-destruct in a buzzing, crackling, electrical shower of guilt and illogic.

"For instance," Paul goes on without a hint of defensiveness, "if I were to live a completely pure lifestyle, then I wouldn't be able to do any of the things that I wanted to do, because, for one thing, I wouldn't fly an airplane. I wouldn't drive a car. If you don't use these forms of transportation, then you might as well just shut up and crawl into a hole, because nobody's ever going to hear anything you have to say." He pauses to rub the dark stubble along his lower jaw.

"You have to use whatever is in your environment. If you live in the jungle, then you use the materials in the jungle. If you live in the city, then you use the tools in the city. A car is a reality to Los Angeles, whereas a llama might be a reality to the Andes."

Agile and even charming, Paul is not the Sea Shepherd officer who tends to get in trouble with more stringent environmentalists. It was Peter who for months lived under extreme disapproval, held in contempt by an impassioned Sea Shepherd staff member after he opposed her animal-rights agenda. The Sea Shepherd Conservation Society, Peter insisted, despite its strong action on behalf of endangered species was not—repeat, *not*—an animal-rights group.

"Hey," says Peter, perhaps a little too cheerfully, "We *eat* animals."

⚓ ⚓ ⚓

Stuart rose early this morning to cook breakfast, but nobody was up except Chris (on watch) and me, so he went back to bed. The exhaustion of the last few days has taken its toll. Soon Chris accepts my offer to finish out her watch, so I'm the only person awake as we plow ahead through the rain. A few days ago I would have paid a thousand dollars for a helicopter to whisk me off the ship. This morning, however, sitting alone on the bridge, socked in with rain and fog, everyone still asleep, I'm glad for some time to sort out my thoughts.

By noon the crew is up and moving about. We're all a bit on edge, wondering what will happen next, and we get our first scare when the *Sea Shepherd II* radar picks up a contact about twelve miles away. Another driftnetter? A Japanese patrol boat? Peter says we won't waste much time if it's a driftnetter. Just bump and run. As the mystery ship gets within range of the *Edward Abbey*'s radar, Paul thinks the image looks too large for a driftnetter, but the grey rain has so diminished our visibility that we won't see it until it's right on top of us. On radar the ship appears to be heading directly at us, so we should know soon.

As Meg, Stuart, Peter, Paul and I crowd the bridge, a huge cargo ship moves toward us, crossing our bow perhaps a quarter-mile ahead, a mountainous platform of consumer goods slipping through the white-grey fog. It looks like an unmoored island. With binoculars Paul sees signs of Mexican registry. He radios a Jimmy duty to the *Sea Shepherd II* asking for some information about the ship, and Jimmy dutifully talks to them in Spanish.

"They're heading for Long Beach," he radios back to Paul after an extended discussion.

If so, they are going in exactly the wrong direction. With utter composure, as if nothing could matter less, Jimmy says that he probably got the information backward.

⚓ ⚓ ⚓

"Dance, beautiful wench! Tomorrow you may betray me, as I know you will. But tonight I watch you dance."

Stuart repeats his favorite three sentences from *Conan the Barbarian* so often that everyone knows them by heart. A game has developed—without anyone calling it a game—that requires finding a suitable occasion to summon your best east European gutturals and growl out, "Dance, beautiful wench!"

At first Meg and Chris provide the obvious occasions, but soon they, too, begin growling—directing the command at male crew members—which of course ultimately unleashes verbal and gender anarchy: anyone, anytime, is likely to be addressed as a beautiful wench and commanded to dance. A Conan epidemic sweeps the ship. For some reason the order to start dancing works particularly well on Scamp.

This spoof of comic-book manliness, however feeble, typifies a welcome rise in spirits. Everyone's thoughts begin to turn toward home. Meg, Ken and I—the nonsailors onboard—plan a beeline to the nearest public transportation. Stuart wonders whether breaking the lease on his new Corvette will disqualify him for student aid, which says something about student life in the 1990s. Peter works on developing and editing film for delivery to the TV networks. Paul plans a couple of news conferences. Otherwise it's just another rainy, gloomy day, with only a tricky refueling operation scheduled to break up the greyness. A stray albatross and a storm petrel pass by on their way somewhere else.

Spirits begin to lag, however, as the day stretches on. I give up waiting for my wet jeans to dry—some five days after I washed them in saltwater. (Joy dishwashing liquid, I'm told, is the preferred brand for washing clothes in saltwater, but of course we have only an inept generic substitute.) Bracing for derision, I spend about forty minutes on the bridge slowly hand-turning the jeans in front of a tiny electric space heater. Nobody seems to notice. The air is so heavy with all-permeating dampness that even the pages of a book feel too limp for reading.

We're headed to a port called Tofino, on Vancouver Island, and I'm wondering how I'm supposed to get home from there, wherever that is. Well, Conan wouldn't worry. He'd just look around for a beautiful wench to growl at. He knows she'll betray him, but it doesn't matter. Wandering through a world of slavers, magicians, snow apes, pirates, enemies on every side, many of them scantily clad beautiful women trying to kill him, he confronts his fate with a pure barbarian candor: "I love, I slay and am content."

He's a decent sort of barbarian, old Conan, and I come to like him, black-haired, sullen-eyed, possessing the strength of twelve ordinary men. He's a warrior and a man of action, moving through the chaos with unerring instincts. The three

Conan comic books onboard are duplicates from Paul's full run of the original series, which he started buying as a kid. His collection of *Conan the Barbarian*, he says, is probably his most valuable possession.

⚓ ⚓ ⚓

The Brits have requested permission to do a day's filming onboard the *Edward Abbey*. We strongly suspect that what they really want, desperately, is a day off from vegan cooking. Peter, filming onboard the *Sea Shepherd II*, spots Sam on deck with his omnipresent vegan bowl.

"Rice and beans?" he asks. "Or is it beans and rice?"

"Not funny," Sam replies.

One of the Brits complains that a rat has eaten his favorite T-shirt. Another has lost a bottle of rum. The Brits, too, must be thinking about home, counting the days until they can sit in the warmth of a local pub.

Paul realizes that everyone's mind is elsewhere. Perhaps that's why, on the bridge, he gives a surprisingly dramatic reading of some key passages in Castaneda's *Tales of Power*. Stuart has asked to borrow Paul's copy, but Paul instead flips to a passage he thinks might interest Stuart and begins to read aloud. The passage, as I might have guessed, concerns the *nagual*.

Don Juan is explaining to Castaneda that everything we believe to be real constitutes a kind of inventory of the world. Searching for an example, he says that our minds contain an inventory of the world, much as glasses, silverware and dishes constitute an inventory of what is on a restaurant table. Thus trees and rocks and airplanes belong to our inventory of the world, but so do ideas. Everything we can think of or imagine sits on the world table, like so many spoons and forks.

Is the idea of God part of the real?

Yes, Don Juan explains. God is an especially big idea, maybe like the entire tablecloth, but it, too, belongs to our world inventory, a portion of whatever is nameable and conceivable.

By contrast, the *nagual* is like the empty space beyond the table. The empty space represents immense and powerful forces that we have no language for, no way to understand. The *nagual* exceeds all our abilities to conceive of it. But don't make the mistake of thinking it's unreal simply because we can't name it or think about it. The earth holds far more than the contents of our minds.

Although Paul is supposedly reading these passages to Stuart, nearly the entire crew has drifted onto the bridge, hunching onto the tabletops or loitering near the open stairwell leading to the radio room. Paul knows he has an audience, and he responds with a dazzling performance, like some ancient mariner pulled out of a time warp. Perhaps he's reminding us, obliquely, that the normal world we long for—Ann Arbor, Portland, Santa Monica—is not all there is. We name it, feel it, almost taste it, but meanwhile a far more powerful reality, unseen and unnamed, moves through the world like deep ocean currents, around us and under us and through the bridge of the *Edward Abbey*, if we only knew it.

⚓ ⚓ ⚓

At 4:30 in the afternoon, as I sit on the bridge substituting for Peter—who has at last run critically short of sleep—I hear an unusual throbbing sound. Suddenly a large white four-engine plane with red and orange insignia drops from the solid grey cloud cover and flies straight toward the *Edward Abbey*.

Alarmed, I shout for Peter, who, dazed with exhaustion, leaps from his bunk and scrambles to the bridge with his shoulder-mounted camera. Then I run to summon Paul in the galley, where he has lingered to tell a few more afternoon stories. He receives my news with unconcern.

"Oh, yeah. It's probably the Coast Guard. They check on us from time to time."

Maintaining a casual air, Paul nonetheless walks to the bridge as the plane circles for a second pass. He picks up the mike hanging from its ceiling hook and tries to make radio contact.

He's right. It's a U.S. Coast Guard plane out of Kodiak Island, Alaska, about nine hundred miles north.

"The government of Japan has filed a complaint with the U.S. State Department," the pilot says. "They say that the *Sea Shepherd II* and the *Edward Abbey* endangered one of their fishing vessels by acting in a grossly negligent manner."

The pilot sounds a little stiff, as if he's reading from an official report. I'm relieved it's not a Japanese plane. The politeness, or at least the formality, of the pilot's speech strikes me as odd. He asks us what happened and what our destination is.

Paul replies with equal formality that he is full owner of the *Sea Shepherd II*, which he leases to the Sea Shepherd Conservation Society, and that the Sea Shepherd Conservation Society is the listed owner of the *Edward Abbey*. The Society, he says, takes "full responsibility" for all its actions. He adds that he'll file a complete report when he reaches land. The pilot, apparently satisfied, banks the plane sharply and disappears into the low grey clouds.

"This time they bit!" Paul says, elated.

He and Peter immediately huddle in the radio room to construct a press release: "U.S. COAST GUARD INTERROGATES *SEA SHEPHERD*. JAPANESE DRIFTNETTERS CAUGHT RED-HANDED." Maybe I won't get to Tofino after all.

"You guys worry too much," Paul says to no one in particular. A little later, however, he is poring over the ship's log. Then he radios Jon and asks him to read out the *Sea Shepherd II* log, especially our encounter with the Japanese. Jon hems and haws. Finally he says Paul won't like what he hears. A ship's log, I learn, is a legal document, a faithful record of times, positions and events, but the *Sea Shepherd II* crew have been using it like a diary, entering gossip, limericks, riddles and whatever strikes their fancy. Paul chews out Jon in drill-sergeant language. Eventually Jon has sorted out the log and reads it back over the radio. Paul compares the entries detailing our encounter with the *Gen Ei Maru No. 68* and *No. 79*.

Around dusk I watch as he walks alone to starboard carrying the single-barrel shotgun, which moments later slips noiselessly into the sea.

⚓ ⚓ ⚓

What to make of the events I've just lived through? What troubles me most, it's clear, is the gunfire. Like Meg, I'd thought that Sea Shepherd ships carried weapons only for self-defense. The gunfire that accompanied our attack on the Japanese ships was not defensive. Maybe it was meant to intimidate, to frighten, to send a message, but like any act, it is open to interpretation. Paul probably meant the Japanese captain to interpret the shots as a serious threat: an action-text that might be translated roughly as "These crazies mean business, so let's get out of here!"

But can we control how other people interpret our actions? Could you send the same message without gunfire? Was it a genuine threat—a prelude to possible attack—or just an elaborate, noisy bluff? Is there any meaningful difference between a threat and a bluff? The questions keep piling up.

Paul is a master of the strategic bluff—or threat. In March 1983, for example, he positioned the *Sea Shepherd II* at the mouth of the harbor in St. John's, Newfoundland, to blockade the Canadian seal fleet. He insists that he had no intention of attacking, but he announced publicly that he would ram the first sealing ship that left the harbor. His record of ramming ships gave credibility to the announcement, and the first rule of a successful bluff is that you must be credible. No ships left the harbor that season, and some seventy-six thousand seals escaped slaughter.

The art of successful bluffing requires that no one except the bluffer know for sure whether it's real. A good bluff either misleads your opponent or generates deep uncertainty. That's what bothers me. People sometimes take impulsive steps and make terrible mistakes when they feel threatened and uncertain.

Paul seems pleased at the fear we inspired. The Sea Shepherd Conservation Society—with its helter-skelter volunteer crew—has made its way past innumerable difficulties to come out here and confront the driftnetters. Who else would do it? Paul knows his methods aren't gentle, and he isn't looking for praise, at least not from people alive today. Environmentalists, he says, make great ancestors.

Earlier on the trip he told me about a man who approached him on a peace march in Vancouver a few months after Rod Coronado and David Howitt had shut down the Icelandic whaling fleet.

"I just wanted to let you know that what you people did in Iceland was reprehensible, criminal, deplorable and totally unforgivable," the man told Paul. He continued his tirade with a series of articulate, impassioned condemnations.

Paul waited patiently until the man had finished.

"What's your name?" he asked his surprised accuser. The man replied that his name was John.

"Well, John," Paul said, "when we planned this campaign, we didn't sit around and ask ourselves, 'I wonder what John's gonna think if we sink these ships, or maybe we should ask John what his opinion is.' Frankly, John, we don't give a damn what you or anybody else on this planet thinks. We didn't sink those ships for you. We did it for the whales. It's the whales we care about, John. Not you."

CHAPTER TWELVE

WHAT TO DO

• • •

Another grey, grey day. The rain lets up, only to start again. The most immediate threat now seems death by mildew. The sea and air appear to form a single element—or maybe a twilight zone—not just indifferent to human desires but utterly alien, inhuman and inherently hostile. Nothing out here remains of the familiar world that human beings have built up lovingly over the last forty thousand years. One unlucky step and you drop into that endless rocking grey, without a marker, lungs choked with salt and bones picked clean by undersea scavengers. The weather today puts you on notice that nature doesn't care about your well-being. Live or die: it doesn't matter to the sea.

Sue and Myra, friends since their undergraduate years at the University of California, visit Paul aboard the *Edward Abbey* for a private talk about the fate of the *Sea Shepherd II*. Their severe pulled-back hair and soiled engine-room garb impart a no-nonsense air. Serious, competent, fierce, willing to die for their beliefs, they'll get what they want, and it's rumored that Sue's wealthy parents might come up with money to buy the *Sea Shepherd II*. Talk has continued about a campaign against the revived Icelandic whaling fleet. One scenario would outfit the *Sea Shepherd II* with an all-female crew, no doubt headed by Myra and Sue, who would not only sink the whaling fleet but hand the patriarchal Icelanders a public relations nightmare.

Trevor, without a prayer, argues that Paul should give the ship to him. Peter, meanwhile, places a call to a rich backer who has suggested turning the ship into an environmental museum, but somehow big plans always come unglued when it's time to pay up.

Will Paul decide to sink the *Sea Shepherd II* on the voyage in—like the old doomed warrior going down in a final fight, the aged Beowulf against the dragon? His private talk with Myra and Sue continues for quite a while, delaying their zodiac ride back to the *Sea Shepherd II.* As the waves rise, Myra struggles with the instant seasickness that afflicts visitors to the *Edward Abbey*, afterward hanging out in Peter's vacant bunk to await the zodiac.

Over slip-sliding bowls in the galley, Stuart, Jim and I conduct a postlunch seminar. Is the global climate really changing? Our discussion is significant mainly in that somewhere a thousand miles out in the wild North Pacific, on a small pitching cutter, three adults earnestly sit down to argue whether the world is heating up. A sign of the times. Also significant: carbon dioxide, nitrous oxide, methane and other greenhouse gases trap incoming heat from the sun. If enough greenhouse gases get into the air as a byproduct of cars, burnt-out rain forests, rice paddies, wars and, yes, even termites and flatulent cows, then we will have changed the air we breathe of the planet. Each day humans pump into the atmosphere some 56 million tons of carbon dioxide. Increased carbon dioxide, regardless of its impact on global warming, speeds up plant growth, with a likely impact on the carbon cycle and nitrogen cycle, promising large-scale ecosystem changes.

As our seminar turns to other topics, I quote the famous, if perhaps inauthentic, statement attributed to Chief Seattle, the nineteenth-century Native American sage: "If all the animals were to vanish, mankind would die from a great loneliness of spirit." Humans may be the first creatures since the lemming to pursue self-extermination. If we have come to view every nonhuman creature from whales to ranch minks as just so much fur or meat or entertainment, we ultimately risk killing off something essential within ourselves. A great loneliness of spirit may be closer than we think.

Stuart talks about traveling to Oregon after we get back and persuading the dean at Lewis and Clark College to accept him as a first-year student in environmental law. They turned down his application a year ago, but maybe now, with more experience and greater confidence, he'd stand a better chance. Like me, he feels that he's not the same person who left Santa Cruz: these days onboard the *Edward Abbey* add up to a mental and emotional sea change. Stuart's eyes brighten as we talk about his plan for starting over in Oregon.

As for Jim, his welding job at the shipyard is gone. It took months to find, months when he was sleeping in his truck and surviving on one bowl of rice a day. He talks about going back to school, asks me what he should study, but it's probably just talk. Not that he doesn't *want* to go back, but somehow it won't happen. Or else he'll leave when the professors don't measure up to his standard. He needs someone to give his drifting, unsettled life a bedrock. I guess, in that case, I'd wish for him someone as strong and lovely as Ruth. I'd wish him—is it impossible these days?—a steady job in a town surrounded by deep woods, with a clear stream running behind his cabin.

The proposed campaign to Iceland sounds serious. As he leaves with the zodiac to pick up Sue and Myra, Trevor radios Paul to ask if he can stay onboard the *Sea Shepherd II* when it makes its assault on the Icelandic fleet. Knowing that his sister wants Trevor to finish high school, Paul refuses.

"Be nice to him, Paul," Sue urges a bit later. "Trevor's really upset."

"I told him I'd be nice when he stopped smoking," replies Paul, who has never touched a cigarette.

Sue reminds Paul that he ran away to sea, implying that he ought to understand Trevor's impatience.

"I had no choice," Paul replies.

It looks like a family tradition.

⚓ ⚓ ⚓

After a hard night, little by little the sun appears. Not a brilliant, blazing sun, but enough to burn away the dank and gloom, leaving the sky pale blue and streaked with flat, white clouds. As if to confirm the change, four orca whales swim by about half a mile off the port side. Later a pod of Dall's porpoises begins to play close around the ship, diving then suddenly rising, cutting the surface with their rounded backs and sharklike fins in a fluid, up-down, carousel rhythm. Dall's porpoises are actually a species of dolphin, but their black backs and white bellies give them the appearance of miniature killer whales. We all run for our cameras.

The weather inside my head is mixed. I phone Ruth and ask her to check the flights from Vancouver. Surprisingly, Peter gets a connection almost immediately because a group of helpful ham radio operators are monitoring our signals. They seem to know something is up. Is the FBI or Canadian Coast Guard waiting to ask questions—or worse? Could a Japanese complaint to the State Department get us arrested? Paul keeps saying that Tokyo pulls the strings in Washington, which is why we're headed to Vancouver Island.

In an attempt to reassure me, Peter adds that under maritime law the ship—not the crew—is held responsible for any misdeeds, an idea I find preposterous, which probably means that Peter is correct. I remain skeptical, though. Paul's Kafkaesque warning spins in my mind: "Always maintain a healthy paranoia."

A Canadian military aircraft flies low over the ship about noon. So much for paranoia.

Still, Paul is an antidote for the worries that seep into whatever frontal lobe keeps us focused on the future. The way of the warrior, he says, provides what you need. Once, in December 1986, the *Sea Shepherd II* pulled into the south of England after a severe battering. Paul had no money for the badly needed repairs. That night he dreamed he had dinner with the wealthy owner of the Falmouth shipyards, whose yacht just happened to be riding at anchor nearby. Next morning Paul wrote a letter to the owner and hand-delivered it to the first mate. The owner wasn't around, but the first mate faxed the letter to London and almost immediately received instructions to give Paul whatever he needed at no cost.

Dreams and visions matter to Paul. He seems to regard them not as enigmatic communications from a buried or repressed layer of the self—that poor, shriveled postmodern ghost—but as a fuller and wiser speech issuing from the earth. Dreams and visions also seem to come when they are needed, as at Wounded Knee. There, at the site where in 1890 U.S. troops massacred some two hundred mostly unarmed Sioux Indians, women and children alike, Paul was guided through a sweat lodge ceremony by Wallace Black Elk, grandson of the famous medicine man Black Elk. In the small rounded hut covered with buffalo skin, the steam from red-hot rocks sent the temperature so high that Paul felt himself slipping in and out of consciousness.

Then he saw a pool of clear water, and in the water he saw his own reflection: a grey wolf. (Hence his Lakota name: Grey Wolf Clear Water.) He saw, too, a single buffalo on a hillside. Arrows trailing long strings came shooting out of the distance and struck the buffalo. Suddenly Paul felt himself running toward the source of the shots. He was running so low to the ground that he knew he must be a wolf. Racing up to one of the hunters, he leaped to rip out the man's throat. Just before his jaws clamped shut, he stopped, turned and ran back to the dying buffalo.

As Paul later thought about the vision, he realized that whales are the buffalo of the sea. In fact they originated as land animals millions of years ago, which is why they still must rise to the surface to breathe. The stringed arrows were harpoons. The lesson of the grey wolf—seizing the hunter by the throat and then releasing him—is that you must frighten the oppressors, but not hurt them.

Powerful visions appear so often throughout history that you would think we'd eventually take them seriously—if only as a statistical phenomenon. Many religions embrace visionary experience, from American Indian shamanism to Hebrew prophecy to Christian mysticism. A supernatural source isn't required to explain all visions: they can be induced through various natural or artificial hallucinogens, ascetic rituals or a sweat lodge ceremony. What matters is not what induced the vision but whether the vision communicates a truth powerful enough to change us.

Paul tells of a Norwegian harpooner who said that he had never thought much about killing whales. It was just a job. Now, he said, after Paul had made him stop and see—really look at—what he was doing, he would be happy to join the *Sea Shepherd II* on its next campaign.

Maybe it's not more electronic images or mind bombs that we need but rather a few powerful visions. The power to change comes ultimately only from within us. We can envision a world in harmony with nature, and possibly we can change in ways that will achieve it. Or are Western consumers now so estranged from nature that nothing we experience can make us rethink what our relation to the natural world might be like if we laid down our credit cards and harpoons?

⚓ ⚓ ⚓

The sun didn't last, and now the seas have turned very rough and choppy. It is a dull day, passed mostly in idleness, as I retreat to my bunk, sweating, with the familiar seasick knot in the pit of my stomach that makes conversation difficult. Our eagerness to get home is mocked by our slow, plodding pace. Peter shoots more film and spends hours hunched over his video editing equipment. A Canadian Coast Guard plane on a training run—so they claim—drops out of the clouds for a closer look. The Coast Guard has a long history of keeping track of Paul.

I'm feeling beat up by the constant rocking. It's a battle each morning to brush my teeth as the ship's motion slams me against the narrow walls of the head. No one wants to empty the canister of soiled toilet paper, and the stench filters into our adjoining cabin. My clothes have the texture of damp rags. After some nineteen days trapped together in this tiny lurching box, we are all coming a bit unglued. Stuart and I sit down in the galley for a face-to-face talk across the narrow Formica tabletop, but it's too difficult. The sliding, clattering, tumbling kitchenware and windowless imprisonment give us both a dose of nausea. We look at each other, gesture hopelessly and give up. Solitude is better today than strangling a crewmate in rage and frustration.

Meanwhile the seas turn so rough that Paul decides it's best to cast off the towline connecting us to the *Sea Shepherd II*. We're close enough to reach land under our own power, and we'll ride smoother if we're not towed. Besides, it's doubtful whether the repaired towrope can stand the strain. Then, as night falls, the dim outline of a ship appears on the horizon. It makes no response to our repeated radio calls. The constant pounding has brought us all to the point where no one really wants to think about what it might mean.

⚓ ⚓ ⚓

The day begins for me at 5:30 A.M. when I hear a loud knock at Paul's door. No one wakes Paul before breakfast unless it's an emergency. I can't hear the exchange, but I bolt upright and out of my sleeping bag in record time. I've learned how to get dressed in the dark without waking Meg, but today the violence of the rocking reduces me to sitting on the hard floor as I pull on my jeans. There's no incentive to linger on the littered, damp, grease-stained throw rug. Stumbling to the bridge, almost attacked by the door frame, I notice that the seas have gotten even rougher. I've never seen such immense waves.

The *Edward Abbey* is climbing up huge, grey, rolling hills of water and then plunging down into the troughs. As we climb toward the crest of another massive wave, I see a large white vessel heading straight toward us. My hopes for getting home take another dive.

The U.S. Coast Guard ship *Resolute*, out of Astoria, Oregon, radios an order that we must prepare to be boarded. The *Resolute* looks like an ocean liner, glossy, serene, majestic—but with gun turrets. As an American ship, even though in international waters, the *Edward Abbey* has to obey. Paul looks more alert than normal, at least for early morning, although still calm. When he rams a ship, he says, it's as if everything shifts into slow motion. Life has produced an experience so absolute and intense that it occurs not in quick successive moments but in lingering panoramas.

The high seas make every movement difficult—no panoramas for me—but the *Resolute* has nonetheless launched a jumbo zodiac that holds about ten men clad in bright orange and black, pistols strapped to their belts. As they reach us and climb aboard, I admire their expensive, high-tech jumpsuits, which can turn into inflatable life preservers at the pull of a ripcord. The two men left to pilot the zodiac, which continues to circle around the *Edward Abbey* like a squad car, wear regulation hard hats and communicate by radio with the boarding party and the captain onboard the *Resolute*. We learn that it has a crew of eighty, three lounges and five TV sets. Big screen, no doubt.

The Coast Guard has really got this seafaring business figured out. While the *Edward Abbey* bucks up and around and down on every wave, the *Resolute* sits in the water like a gentleman in an armchair savoring an after-dinner cigar.

These are cops, however, orange-and-black sea cops, and mistrust quickly stamps out my envy. One officer with a trim blonde mustache plants himself on the bridge and smiles excessively, trying to dig out information with transparent small talk. Just looking at him makes me want to lie about everything. Passing through the bridge, Scamp mutters under his breath that he "ain't saying nothing without a lawyer. I got in trouble that way once." Dawn is no more than a dark smudge on the horizon.

It doesn't take long to figure out what Scamp is muttering about. While most of the boarding party splits up to search the ship—ostensibly to check for safety violations—the officers set up shop in the galley. Starting with Paul, at intervals they call each member of the crew, one by one, down to the galley. I'm almost last, and the first words I hear from the officer consist of my Miranda rights.

This is the first time I've been told I have the right to remain silent, to consult a lawyer and that anything I say can be used against me in a court of law. The last phrase gives me a momentary shudder. My mind races. Maybe I'm not guilty of anything so far, but false testimony is a crime. Should I ask for a lawyer? They'll assume I have something to hide, which could tie me up for months in legal runarounds. On the other hand, I have no intention of incriminating anyone, including myself. My loyalties are not to the law but to Paul and the crew of the *Edward Abbey*. Moreover, under no circumstances will I hand over my journal or tapes, although a refusal might well land me in jail. So do I swear I'll tell the truth—and risk the legal consequences of a false statement or withholding evidence? The Coast Guard team awaits my reply.

"What did you do?" I ask Peter, who is sitting at the table like an interpreter.

Peter flashes me a bright, impenetrable grin. "I told them everything they want to know," he says.

And so the interview begins. The questions come from a sheet no doubt faxed to the *Resolute* by some poor devil of a clerk in the basement of the State Department. Your name? Where do you live? What do you do for a living? How close did the *Sea Shepherd II* come to the Japanese vessel?

I answer casually, fortified by my recall of Huck Finn's fine American distinction between outright lies and "stretchers." But I don't need stretchers because the interrogators ask only very specific questions about what I saw. Who can dispute what I say I saw? The rest I bury in silence. The interview ends with a request for permission to take a photograph. I look into the camera, summon up a thin smile and hope that we don't get ordered to follow the *Resolute* back to Oregon.

My smile comes partly from recognizing that the Coast Guard team—accustomed to its luxurious quarters—is turning grey-green with seasickness in the cluttered, windowless galley. They want to be off this bouncing ship as much as I do.

Peter Brown and Paul Watson share their duties with a sense of politeness, irony and theater.

Peter hastens the conclusion when, with another inscrutable grin, he offers to hand over a videotape of the confrontation with the *Gen Ei Maru No. 79*. "No charge," he says breezily. Peter doesn't tell them that he has much more videotape—and better, too. The Coast Guard gets what anybody gets: an edited version. In a similarly expansive gesture, Paul passes out a handful of round Sea Shepherd arm patches bearing the logo "Neptune's Navy." Never have the captain and first mate carried out their joint duties with a finer mix of politeness, irony and theater. The sailors look just out of high school. As we tell them about our mission, two or three ask how to join up when their hitch expires. I get the impression that even the interrogators are merely doing a job. No one out here likes driftnetters.

By 10:00 A.M., when the Coast Guard crew prepares to climb into their waiting zodiac, the seas have gotten so rough that once again the rope ladder at the stern of the *Edward Abbey* dangles uselessly, sometimes six or eight feet above the waves. One by one the crew members drop into their pitching zodiac as buddies grab at their legs. They at least get paid for this. Meg is ashen with seasickness, while I survive by popping Dramamine tablets every few hours. Mister Toad's Wild Ride, with puking, no lines and no tickets.

What's really galling is that for the past four hours the Coast Guard has made us cut our speed. To keep from capsizing, we have to steer the *Edward Abbey* directly into the waves, due west. Each hour thus adds not just sixty minutes of delay but sixty minutes of moving backward. At least two hundred miles of towering swells and whitecaps now stand between us and land. A tree would hold almost erotic attractions right now.

But it's not over. The *Resolute* radios that it is a violation of U.S. law for Paul, as the citizen of a foreign country, to captain a U.S. registered vessel. Paul patiently explains that the Coast Guard at Long Beach waived this provision because the *Edward Abbey* is commissioned for research, but the captain of the *Resolute* is, well, resolute. He orders Paul not to leave Vancouver Island without paperwork establishing a U.S. citizen as captain of the *Edward Abbey*. The exchange of technicalities is no more than a bland nuisance. I'm guessing that the real object of the Coast Guard search was drugs, since they missed some pretty obvious safety violations. Drugs, as it happens, are taboo on Sea Shepherd campaigns. Paul once found out that a crew member was using drugs and dropped him at a port in the middle of nowhere.

"I mean, like, don't I get a second chance?" the guy asked.

"No," said Paul.

Finally the *Resolute* disappears over the rolling horizon. As we all uncoil for the first time in hours, Paul turns the *Edward Abbey* around, pumps up the engines and we plunge ahead toward whatever awaits us.

⚓ ⚓ ⚓

With its twin diesel engines running flat out, the noise aboard the *Edward Abbey* is too deafening for conversations more than a few words long. I spend my time silently on the bridge, where Meg, not only recovered but looking almost robust, is steering us confidently up and down waves so huge that they lift the stern clear out of the water. At such moments, with the propellers fanning air, the wheel is completely useless and we move wherever the sea puts us down. Meg steers casually with one hand, her feet propped up like a chief executive. Any one of these massive swells could flip us over, so hanging around the bridge doesn't give me peace of mind. Most of the crew have gone off to find semiprivate spots where they can endure the racket and pummeling without the effort that conversation requires. I take to my bunk to write.

In the comforting, open-door twilight of my cabin, I think back to Paul, on camera, when Peter asked him what the average person can do to help protect the environment. His response surprised me: "Do what you do best."

Then, sensing that Peter wanted something a little more expansive and specific, he added a few concrete examples.

"If you're a teacher, teach. If you're a builder, build. If you're a writer, write. But do whatever you do best with a constant awareness of whether your impact on the environment is positive or negative."

Paul's words help me make sense of this journey. Not everyone can be an activist, someone who stirs things up, provokes confrontations, unsettles the opposition, rams ships. The term Paul employs for such people is *catalyst,* and he clearly enjoys his catalytic role. Stubborn, dedicated and compelling, he was born for the spotlight, with a nerve equal to the challenge. He has a big ego—the job requires it—but he's far from egotistical. Just bold, confident and outgoing. Once, after locating her name in a library phone book, he placed a long-distance call to the *Playboy* Playmate of the Month and talked for several hours. Flight attendants hit on him in airplanes.

He knows he draws attention, but when he's not confronting enraged sealers or debating government ministers, he can also reveal a surprising gentleness. This gentleness is worth emphasizing because one danger of his radical activism is that it can alienate moderate, law-abiding, gentle people who share his concern for the earth. It's a danger he accepts. He is a rebel who doesn't want or expect praise. Those moderate, law-abiding people—like me—need to know that gentleness and moderation alone will not protect the earth against industrialists, lawyers, developers and corrupt officials who exploit every last available quantum of natural resources. These qualities won't protect the earth against all us moderate, gentle people with our two-car garages and our lawn sprinklers and our energy-fat appliances.

People *need* to be confronted when the alternative is to go on sleepwalking gently into the abyss.

So what about those of us who don't have the temperament or the conviction to be catalytic, ship-ramming activists?

In *Earthforce!* Paul describes five other roles that the Earth Warrior can assume: healer, communicator, artist, infiltrator and shaman. When I asked him which role best described him, he upset my expectations, as usual, and replied that he didn't know yet. I interpret his reply not as modesty but as a reminder of the open-ended, unfinished, ongoing quality of human life. How do we know what we are capable of? Paul Watson may yet perform almost every role possible in defense of the earth. More important, his response suggests that we can all move in directions that may not seem clear yet or even possible. His ultimate role is perhaps to help us imagine that we can live in a very different relation to nature. As poet William Blake wrote, "What is now proved was once only imagined."

I also draw some hope from what I might call the "environmental paradox." It's similar to the infamous hermeneutic circle: you can't understand a part until you understand the whole, but you can't understand the whole until you understand the parts. Understanding is thus logically impossible, but nonetheless goes on all the time. Perhaps nothing we do as separate individuals will have a significant impact on protecting the earth. The earth will be truly protected, however, only when individuals, in their insignificant separateness, begin to act.

⚓ ⚓ ⚓

With the engines roaring and the ship nearing land, I find myself thinking about Trevor and about how, in the patriarchal Anglo-Saxon era, in the time of Beowulf, the most important bond was the relation between nephew and uncle—particularly between a young man and his mother's brother. An Anglo Saxon was never absolutely sure about his biological father, but he always knew his mother's brother. Even today, uncles usually escape from the oedipal conflicts that bedevil fathers and sons. There are other conjectures, but I like to think that "to cry uncle" refers to the time when young men, like Trevor, would test themselves not against their fathers but against the other immediate male relative who had the unspoken duty to teach and protect him.

What sparked these thoughts was a long debate last night over the ship's radio, when Trevor argued with Paul about whether he needed to complete high school. Paul ran through the standard defenses of education—somewhat unconvincingly, I thought—adding for Trevor's benefit the ingenious argument that a radical environmentalist needs a knowledge of machines, for example, in order to sabotage them. Trevor shot back that he could learn all he needed to know about machines by reading instruction manuals and working as a mechanic. How did Paul know that he hadn't sabotaged plenty of machines already?

So it went, for more than an hour back and forth—with neither uncle nor nephew giving ground. It was a duel that Paul didn't intend to lose, of course, and his promise to his sister made the outcome inevitable. Trevor, however, held his own. As usual he was overmatched, but not crushed or even clearly defeated. The debate ended in a draw. It seemed that the balance of power had just subtly shifted, and maybe Paul even secretly felt pleased with the unexpected mental acuity of his opponent. Trevor didn't need more schooling to learn how to argue.

The nighttime exchange also reminded me of a story Paul told. His unscheduled sparring matches with Trevor sometimes go on for extended periods, long after an ordinary kid would have cried uncle. When he grew tired or just decided to end it, Paul could stop the duels almost at will by using his Aikido training. The first mate on one of the *Sea Shepherd II* campaigns, after watching Paul beat up on Trevor, made the mistake of trying the same thing. Trevor left him so bruised that he didn't come out of his cabin for three days.

A new generation of activists is growing up. In one sense, Paul has trained them, or at least offered a model and created an organization to give them experience they will need elsewhere. Like high-schooler Rod Coronado traveling to Vancouver to meet his hero, nearly every young activist must know who Paul Watson is. His life sets a powerful example. In another sense, however, the new generation of activists may not observe his rule—"Frighten the oppressors but do not harm them"—especially if they see that the earth continues to be devastated by forces even Paul Watson couldn't overcome. In that case, Earth Warriors of Trevor's generation may see their only options as principled destruction or unprincipled destruction. They can cynically join the destroyers, do nothing or blow them up.

Paul doesn't expect success. "You do what you can do," he says, "that's all."

Sometimes he speaks as if the only hope lies in just buying time so a few more whales and wolves and redwoods can survive to reproduce before an apocalypse frees the earth from human domination. I hope he's wrong. Like whales and wolves and redwoods, humans belong to the earth. We, too, are the product of millions of years of evolution. Our greatest gift is doubtless the consciousness that permits us to reflect upon our place within nature. The best hope for circumventing Paul's doomsday scenarios may be simply to reflect long and deeply on what it means to belong to the earth—before time runs out.

Success in changing the course of human history, however, is not an issue for Paul. His only failure would lie in the failure to act.

⚓ ⚓ ⚓

Tomorrow morning we should strike land. Peter is still readying his videotapes to race to the networks. Paul is arranging for a press conference in Vancouver, followed by a second conference in L.A.—with the requisite celebrities. He makes many of the arrangements over the radiophone with his ex-wife, Starlet Lum, who lives on Vancouver Island with their daughter, Lani. He sounds like any indulgent father as he talks with Lani about the dog she hopes for, a greyhound. With Lani, he doesn't so much abandon his objection to pets as offer a choice. She can get a greyhound, he tells her, or accompany him on a trip to Europe. Like the father of any twelve-year-old, he probably knows, which she will choose.

Even with my anxieties about tomorrow's encounter with Canadian and American authorities, even with my incessant scheming for a speedy cross-country route back to Ruth, I find my thoughts circling back to Paul's response when the Coast Guard plane relayed the Japanese charges that he had endangered lives by operating his ship in a "reckless" manner.

"That wasn't reckless," Paul replied. "I did it on purpose. I hit ships all the time."

EPILOGUE

• • •

Early morning. No one up yet except Paul. He claims you can smell land before you see it, so I step outside the bridge and suck in several deep breaths. I guess I don't have the nose for it. The radar and radio agree, however, that land is near. Finally, after twenty-one days surrounded by empty horizon, I make out the unmistakable shoreline with its thick dark mass of trees. It makes me feel a little dizzy, as if the top of my head has begun to float free.

In colonial New England, Cotton Mather warned about the devils, dragons and fiery flying serpents hidden in the primeval forest. So the Puritan mind had to destroy the forest in order to rid the world of demons. Fortunately, Mather never got to Vancouver Island, although the timber companies did. From an airplane the dense forest looks like a landscape of bomb craters. As we approach by sea, however, the wooded shore of Vancouver Island—half-concealed in the smoky morning mist—holds a beauty so rich and mysterious that my whole body aches.

It seems as if we are entering an enchanted world. The feeling of unreality grows as we thread past uninhabited offshore islets where tall rugged pines grip down onto bare grey rock. Several full-cheeked puffins fly across our bow, like miniature airborne penguins with a dash of color. Paul is talking on the radio with Jon, discussing, a little impatiently, where the *Sea*

Shepherd II should anchor to avoid both expensive pilot fees and possibly hostile authorities. He has already shifted the *Edward Abbey*'s arrival from Tofino to an even smaller port called Ucluelet.

When Paul cuts our engine speed, the early morning quiet gives the impression that we're the only people alive. The smooth, black water continues to grow even calmer until at last the surface resembles a dark still pool. I half expect to see a lone dryad or faun slipping furtively through the woods. A few minutes later, however, we are completely surrounded.

Boats from Canadian Customs and Immigration, the Canadian Coast Guard and the Canadian Royal Mounted Police pull alongside the *Edward Abbey* as we search for the entrance to Ucluelet harbor. Paul certainly draws a welcoming committee. We have no choice but to proceed with our escort. Over the radio, Paul protests repeatedly that its keel is too deep for the shallow channel, but the *Sea Shepherd II*—out of sight and still several hours away—is also summoned to Ucluelet. Soon Paul docks the *Edward Abbey* at a kind of marine warehouse, with the Coast Guard and police boats flanking us on either side.

After three weeks of continuous rocking, the last days a continuous struggle amid engine roar and gigantic swells, the sensation of standing on the motionless deck is dreamlike. The swarm of officials in blue uniforms has us all a little uneasy, so this is not entirely a good dream, but Ken, in a spirit to celebrate, offers a bystander $20 to bring us some soft drinks and chips. All the crew except for Paul and Peter, who are busy with official business, lounge on the aft deck sipping soda. It's as if we've reached Nirvana—with the possibility of imminent arrest.

People in uniform continue to pour through the *Edward Abbey*, searching everywhere. Then, again, we descend one by one to the galley for questioning. Ucluelet consists of a few houses stuck on a low, scarred hill, with maybe a bait shop, but soon a small flotilla of pickup trucks and old cars have pulled up on the opposite bank to watch the spectacle unfold. Everybody here must own police-band radios. I still don't know if we're under arrest. Doesn't anyone ever tell you these things? Finally, after a meticulous search of the *Edward Abbey*, with questioning of the entire crew by the police and processing by Customs and Immigration, in early afternoon I'm the first crew member given permission to depart.

The Canadian officials all refer to me as "the press"—it's useless to explain that I've never practiced ten seconds of professional journalism—but it makes me wonder if my quick clearance means they're eager to get me off the ship. They've been courteous and professional so far. Will it continue after "the press" is gone? But I'm ready to go. The Coast Guard vessel phones nearby Tofino Air, not a major carrier. Its advertisement features a duck in a raincoat. Soon a two-seat seaplane with a duck on its side is skidding to a stop in the narrow harbor.

In one last rite of passage, a Mountie drops my bags onto the RCMP boat. At once, a businesslike German shepherd bounds out from the cabin and begins circling the bags, sniffing. My heart freezes. It hits me that the officials pouring through the *Edward Abbey* easily could have planted a packet of drugs in my gear. The German shepherd keeps sniffing, nose like a crowbar, but at last turns and pads back into the cabin. Elated, with hugs all around, I head for the Coast Guard launch. My legs nearly buckle when the launch deposits me on a slightly unsteady wooden wharf, where the seaplane retrieves me. It all seems too sudden.

With room for almost nothing except the pilot, me and my two bags, the plane taxis down the harbor. I wonder if I'm making a big mistake. I wonder a lot harder as the pilot, head down, struggles to imprint my MasterCard while the plane climbs directly toward the middle of a six thousand-foot mountain. Finally he swoops upward, just in time to clear the pine-strewn rocky peak by a good six feet. When I gratefully stumble out of the seaplane onto a dock at the Vancouver airport, a television crew from the evening news is waiting for me at the end of the gangplank, camera poised.

At the airport, a Canadian Customs and Immigration agent gives my only piece of identification—a Michigan driver's license—a long, very skeptical examination. I have no passport. Nor do I have any idea if I'm wanted for questioning, or worse, in Canada or the United States. My five hours in the Vancouver airport thus include a regular lookout for federal agents. Once ticketed to Detroit, via Seattle and the red-eye to Chicago, I expect to get pulled off the plane and arrested at each stop during my overnight journey back to the Midwest.

As the plane makes its slow descent toward Detroit, where I brace myself to expect a massive industrial grid of concrete and steel, I'm stunned to see dazzling black and silver pools appearing as if by magic in the middle of lush summer cropland. The morning sunlight lends an almost primal innocence to the green, wet earth. It must have been raining for weeks.

Once the plane touches down, I can't quite believe my luck when no one apprehends me and I'm actually free to go home. Ruth is waiting at the gate. Slim when I left, she now looks ten pounds lighter. Maybe the Sea Shepherd Diet Plan works even for spouses. In celebration she has rented a dark blue limo, complete with uniformed driver, and tumbled into a corner of the wide, leather backseat we hold each other like teenagers for the entire thirty-mile ride to Ann Arbor.

Back in Ucluelet, the circus of administrative detail lasts for weeks. The *Edward Abbey* makes it safely back to American waters, but Canada impounds the *Sea Shepherd II* for failure to pay several thousand dollars in pilot fees. Delighted to improvise a solution to his dilemma, Paul decides to abandon the ship in Ucluelet. Later, over the phone, he asks if I recall an O. Henry story entitled "The Ransom of Red Cloud." (The kidnappers, after abducting a child to extort a payoff, finally plead with the parents to take back the unmanageable brat.) The skeleton crew that Paul left on board receives instructions to remove all valuable equipment, in secret, and eventually Paul sells the stripped-down husk. Local arsonists, unaware of the sale but no doubt incensed by the antilogging slogan emblazoned on its hull, firebomb the deck of the *Sea Shepherd II* in an appropriately mindless finale. There's talk that the old hulk will be dragged offshore and sunk to make a reef.

On my return to Ann Arbor I scan two or three newspapers daily for mention of our run-in with the Japanese driftnet fleet. Not a word. Nothing about Japan's official complaint to the State Department. Not a foot of film on the TV evening news. Soon I even stop expecting to find FBI agents on my doorstep. Maybe Peter is right about network news: nobody killed, nothing sunk, no story. When we talk once by phone, he surprises me by saying that he didn't agree with the decision to use guns. He was acting under captain's orders, and he thinks Paul was deliberately escalating the stakes.

But he emphasizes that the shotgun fired harmless "crackers" and the cannon shot off blanks. Even as we talk, I can feel the events begin to blur and fade. I get used to falling asleep with Ruth warm beside me, used to waking up in my own bed, used to brushing my teeth without slamming into the bathroom wall, as the hot days of August turn toward fall.

Paul and I return to far different versions of normal. I have essays and lectures to prepare, while Paul is soon overseeing the purchase of a ship to replace the *Sea Shepherd II*. In a fitting stroke of justice, the replacement is a former driftnet ship impounded for transporting illegal aliens. Paul renames it the *Resolution*, in honor of the UN resolution against driftnet fishing. Its speed should make the next encounter in the North Pacific at least an even match, assuming the water pump is sound. Then in December, Paul takes what Peter described to me as a brief "vacation" in Norway, which, like Iceland, recently announced its intention to resume whaling. It was evidently a working vacation. In December 1992 Paul and several associates, striking from land this time, deftly scuttle the Norwegian whaling ship *Nybræna*.

When we meet again months later, Paul is preparing to sail the *Resolution* into Norwegian waters. Norwegian scientists estimate the number of minke whales worldwide at around 1 million and argue that it no longer constitutes an endangered species. They claim that an annual catch limited to some three hundred minke whales is quite sustainable, especially given plans for traditional coastal whaling in small vessels, unlike the large-scale, open-sea whaling Norway abandoned years ago. IWC scientists agree—although the IWC member nations reject the finding of their own scientific committee. Meanwhile a January 1993 press release announces that the Japanese government and fishing industry will begin separate campaigns encouraging consumers to eat more whale meat. Each month will contain a designated "Whale Meat Eating Day."

It's a complicated issue—raising questions of local custom, party politics, national sovereignty, international jurisdiction—and it's a simple issue: you stop killing whales because it is time for the killing to stop.

A worldwide ban on killing whales is not unthinkable. Like Paul, some countries now believe that whales should not be hunted under any conditions. The coastal states of the Indian Ocean, for example, have asked that the Indian Ocean be declared a permanent sanctuary for whales. The coastal states of the Mediterranean, through the Barcelona Convention, have announced their intention that the Mediterranean be declared a sanctuary for all whales and dolphins. And in May 1994 the forty-member IWC voted to impose a permanent ban on commercial hunting of whales around Antarctica, which puts one-quarter of the world's oceans off-limits to whalers. Only Japan voted against the Antarctica sanctuary. A worldwide ban on killing whales might just be a very good small step—an important symbol, too—in the quest for a better future.

Paul won't wait for the ponderous machinery of diplomats and international commissions to clank through the decision-making process. Whales are being killed and conflict is thus inevitable. His purpose in attacking Norwegian whaling ships is to push up expenses and insurance costs until it is economically unprofitable to kill whales. According to one informant, the prime minister of Norway, respected environmentalist Gro Harlem Brundtland, has privately told the Norwegian police, the military and the Coast Guard to do "whatever is necessary" to stop Sea Shepherd ships.

Such threats have no effect. Paul has since struck again, attempting to sink the Norwegian whaling ship *Senet* outside of Fredrikstad. A spokesperson for the foreign ministry calls it "sabotage bordering on terrorism," indicating that the ministry will ask American authorities to prevent the Sea Shepherd Conservation Society from using its base in California as a jumping-off point for action abroad. Unintimidated, in July 1994 Paul collides with a Norwegian Coast Guard vessel in his newly acquired ship *Whales Forever.* This time it is the Norewegians who do the ramming. As Paul tells it, the Norwegian vessel attacked in international waters using cannon fire and depth charges. The eighteen-hour confrontation left *Whales Forever* battered and leaking oil, but resolute and unbowed. Norway—and other whaling nations—cannot doubt that Paul will continue to apply pressure.

Where threats and attacks fail, some governments may clearly see it in their best interests to cooperate in putting Paul Watson in a position where he cannot trouble them. In March 1994, for example, the Canadian government put Paul on trial in Newfoundland for interfering with a Cuban trawler off the vastly depleted Grand Banks—a trawler Paul claims was both outside Canadian waters and fishing for northern cod, an endangered species. Three of the charges carry a maximum sentence of life imprisonment. If Paul's claims are correct, Canada is engaged in another trumped-up effort to immobilize him in a net of legalism. People always learn faster than governments, however, and the same Newfoundland fishermen who reviled Paul ten years earlier when he opposed the annual seal hunt now cheer him at his arraignment.

"We may lose our ships," Paul writes in the Sea Shepherd log describing an upcoming campaign against Norway, "and ... there is a possibility that one or more of us will make the ultimate sacrifice." He adds, in what I now recognize as the inner calm of someone who feels his existence intimately bound up with the life-dance of the entire earth: "Speaking for myself, this is an acceptable risk."

This is not bravado, fund-raising hype or an inscrutable death wish. It is the measured risk assessment of a veteran activist who knows the cost of opposing powerful forces. He knows the cost because he's been opposing them daily for the last twenty-five years. You cannot do what Paul Watson does, however, and not think at least once in a while about death. As he wrote almost a decade ago, "An epitaph that said I fought to save the whales and the seals and all the creatures of the earth would not be too bad a thing."

Not too bad at all. I expect that Paul will continue to struggle for the earth with all his heart. The battles ahead on the ocean and in the courts seem unending. In the composed way of a warrior, he proceeds with what is perhaps his most unnerving purchase yet: a six-ton, two-person submarine. Built in 1988 and once used by the Norwegian Navy, it is now repainted bright yellow and rides, poised for deployment, on the aft deck of *Whales Forever*. Paul explains that the Sea Shepherd Conservation Society has newly outfitted the sub with stern and bow thrusters, as well as with a mechanical arm used to manipulate tools underwater. The submarine promises valuable help in penetrating harbors for surveillance and enforcement.The possibilities here will occupy his opponents and his supporters into the late, late hours of debate. The ultimate question, in any case, will not be what Paul Watson has accomplished—as in a final balance sheet of actions and achievements—but what we can learn to make of his difficult life's work.

The author sits at his writing post outside the bridge.

ABOUT THE AUTHOR

David Morris grew up in Wilmington, Delaware, where he played a lot of baseball, including a summer of semipro ball, before receiving his B.A. at Hamilton College and his Ph.D. at the University of Minnesota. After spending the 1970s teaching, he resigned his tenured professorship at the University of Iowa in 1982 in order to write. He is the author of numerous scholarly essays and three prize-winning books, most recently *The Culture of Pain* (1991), which was awarded one of the prestigious PEN prizes. He has lectured widely on pain to medical audiences and serves as Associate Editor of the journal *Literature and Medicine*. David has held fellowships from the American Council of Learned Societies, the National Endowment for the Humanities, the National Science Foundation and the Guggenheim Foundation. He lives with his wife, Ruth, in Michigan.

THE SEA SHEPHERD CONSERVATION SOCIETY

FOR MEMBERSHIP OR ADDITIONAL INFORMATION, CONTACT:

Sea Shepherd Conservation Society
3107A Washington Boulevard
Marina del Rey, CA 90292
Tel: (310) 301-7325
Fax: (310) 574-3161